The
Real Estate Way

A Fast Lane Guide to Financial Freedom and
a Secure Retirement

Justin Woodall

Disclaimer

This book is written from the context of my own personal experiences and those that I've observed by being a real estate broker for well over a decade. The scenarios and examples used are just examples. Any given expenses, like repairs, management, taxes, insurance, etc., are estimates. And, I don't always include tax consequences of sales, income tax implications, commissions, fees, etc. To do so would make the examples too confusing and difficult to understand. My goal in the examples is to keep it simple, and their purpose is to teach you how to think. I want you to be able to think and analyze, beyond just "Diversify and hold stocks for the long term," "Invest in your 401K," or "Put money in savings," and hope for the best. The aim is to help you to really evaluate opportunities and see which is best for you and your family. Real estate has accelerated my wealth and passive income much more quickly and easily than I personally could do in stocks or any other way that I know of, other than building a business. I hope it is the beginning of a lucrative and fun journey to building your own portfolio of real estate so that you can be financially free and have more time to spend doing the things you love.

The opinions and statements herein are mine. There is no guarantee that by utilizing the tips, strategies, or information contained in this book you will be profitable. People have made millions in real estate and lost millions in real estate. So, before investing, I recommend that you seek advice of individuals, like CPAs, attorneys, or other people you trust. I am not a CPA, attorney, or financial advisor qualified to give you investing advice. I am a real estate broker licensed in the state of Georgia. Real estate markets are very local, and prices and rents will vary from state to state, city to city, and town to town. So, I recommend you seek the council of trusted advisors before you invest your hard-earned money, but allow this book to entertain you and open your mind to the possibilities of income-producing real estate as a superior way to fund your retirement and your life.

ISBN: 978-1-7339951-0-8

Ninety percent of all millionaires become so through owning real estate. More money has been made in real estate than in all industrial investments combined. The wise young man or wage earner of today invests his money in real estate.

—Andrew Carnegie

FREE RESOURCES

For more resources related to real estate investing, to find a top investment real estate agent in your area or for a link to a **FREE Rental Property ROI Analyzer** tool, visit us online at:

www.TheRealEstateWayBook.com

Contents

INTRODUCTION
The Fast Lane to Financial Freedom through Real Estate

This is not a "get rich quick" book. This book is written for the average person who is tired of the volatility of the stock market and low interest rates paid by savings accounts and CDs. It is for the person who wants financial security and a stable monthly income. It's for the person who wants to be able to retire early! It's for the person who wants to be able to leave assets to their children and grandchildren rather than burn through their retirement savings. It's for the investor who is looking for a more secure, steady, and predictable vehicle that will produce great returns.

Real estate is that vehicle. So many people run away from it because they don't understand it. My aim with this book is to deepen your understanding of real estate, help you determine if it's a vehicle you want to utilize, and be a guide for you as you begin your journey to financial freedom. So, when the title says, "fast lane," it doesn't mean you'll get rich overnight, but the methods in this book can get you to financial freedom much faster than the traditional means of investing in a 401K and a traditional retirement account of stocks and mutual funds.

MANY YEARS AND THOUSANDS OF TRANSACTIONS

I began working in the real estate industry in 2004. At that time, I worked as an individual real estate agent with the largest company in town at that time, Coldwell Banker. Starting out, I was simply helping buyers to buy and sellers to sell real estate. Over time, I met real estate investors and began to see the possibilities and the freedom that income-producing property can deliver to the owners … and to me.

As my past client list grew and demands on my time became greater and greater due to the number of clients that needed my help, I began to grow a team of agents. I then transferred my license to Keller Williams Realty where running and growing a team was a better fit. After spending four years there, I left to open my own real estate business, Woodall Realty Group, and brought my team with me. Our business has grown year over year, and we continue to gain market share in the Athens, Georgia, and surrounding areas. The majority of our business is helping homeowners to buy and sell their primary residences, but we also work with builders and investors. By working in all of the sectors of residential real estate, we have a great overview and understanding of all types of real estate, especially residential.

Through developing this understanding and seeing the possibilities, I, myself, have been able to invest and accumulate income-producing properties that provide a nice annual income for my family and continue to build my wealth. The best thing about it is that the majority of the wealth building is funded by the tenants in my rental properties, rather than out of my own pocket. Because I want you and many, many others to enjoy the same steady income and wealth-building that real estate can provide, I am writing this book. Let's take a moment looking at all you'll learn.

THE REAL ESTATE WAY—AN OVERVIEW

The aim of this book is to show you how you can create your own customized "portfolio" of income-producing real estate to achieve your financial goals, build streams of monthly cash flow, and realize the freedom that can come through real estate.

We'll begin with a comparison of real estate vs. traditional retirement investing, like IRAs and 401Ks, to show the higher returns, the predictability, and the stability that real estate can give in the long-term over these traditional investment routes. We then take a quick look at the work and attitude needed to invest in real estate profitably. For any readers not yet financially set to get started in real estate, I supply some solid recommendations on how to revamp your finances and mindset around money, so that you are prepared to get in the game.

With that groundwork established, we next move into the "what" of real estate investment properties. There are different types of properties you could invest in as well as different classes within each type. We'll look at those and discuss the pros and cons, so you can start figuring out where your interests lie. Next, you'll learn my formula for analyzing a property to determine whether or not it's going to give good returns. Yes, I'm talking return on investment (ROI) here. One key to great returns is finding the right properties. As a long-time real estate agent who also invests in my own properties, I reveal ways to find those hidden gems.

Once you find your deal, you've got to be able to pay for it. You'll learn the traditional means of financing a real estate investment as well as some creative options that can allow you to buy more properties faster and with little or no cash out of your own pocket. Sometimes a little creativity can skyrocket your returns. We'll also discuss the upsides and downsides of different types of ownership.

One bonus of owning real estate is the tax advantages that come along with it. Understanding how to legally take advantage of the tax write-offs can boost your ROI in big ways, so we'll look at this too.

Once you understand the benefits of owning income-producing real estate and determine that it's right for you, in order to really make it work, it must be managed properly. Both the property itself and the tenant must be managed well. This can make or break a real estate investment. We'll look at the costs and benefits of "do it yourself" versus working with a team of professionals and how to scale to the next level. Then we'll consider different types of leasing options that can be utilized in different situations and how to ride the waves of a shifting real estate market. While the value of your real estate may go up or down in a period of years, the annual returns typically will rise consistently regardless of the value—and you'll learn why in this book.

Real estate investing can be a fast lane to financial freedom and a tremendous wealth builder once you see the possibilities and have the belief in yourself that you can make it happen. It can happen faster than most people think. We'll close the book with an examination of the proper mindset for building your portfolio quickly and finding financial freedom.

TAKE CHARGE OF YOUR FUTURE

In a day and time when many people are afraid they may not have enough resources to retire, that their retirement savings may run out, or that the stock market may plummet at the very time they decide to stop working, you don't have to be in that position. Instead, you can be making a consistent and steady income each and every month when you own income-producing real estate. You don't have to live in uncertainty, and you don't have to depend on the government or the whims of world markets to take care of you.

Take charge of your own future, and don't wait to get started! You can make wise choices and decisions when you are equipped with the right information. Learn all you can about the topic. This book is a great place to start learning. Then—take action! With the right knowledge and the right team to help you, it really can happen faster than you can imagine!

If you would like more information or have specific questions on the information provided in this book, you can find me online at any of the following websites:

- www.TheRealEstateWayBook.com

- www.WoodallRealtyGroup.com

- www.Facebook.com/woodallrealtygroup

Turn the page to find out why I believe real estate is your best choice for achieving financial freedom.

CHAPTER 1
Why Real Estate?

Real estate. It's one of those topics almost everyone wants to talk about or is interested in at some level. And since you are reading this book, you are probably one of them. Why is it that real estate seems to have an appeal to so many people? Perhaps because it's real. You can see it, touch it, feel it, walk on it, smell it. It's different from other investments, and it's different from personal property.

MY REAL ESTATE AHA

Real estate has always intrigued me. I did not grow up in a real estate family. My parents owned our house, and my grandfather owned some land that was the old family farm. Otherwise, I didn't know much about it. No one in my family owned any rental property or investment property that produced income.

My parents both worked hard, but what we had came from their toils. It was a family of two working parents who worked hard and gave us all they could. They never made a lot of money, but they made enough. We didn't have designer clothes, shoes, and extravagant vacations, but we had what we needed. We weren't lacking. I never missed a meal, and I was well cared for, but we didn't have extra. I would say that I grew up in a middle-class family in a middle-class neighborhood in Georgia.

I remember when I was in college and I had my first revelation about how lucrative owning real estate and renting it out could be. You know, one of those aha moments. I remember it like it was yesterday. This was the first year that I'd really lived independently of my parents and not in a dorm. I had my own apartment with a roommate and felt like a real adult.

After I placed my monthly rent check into the drop box at my apartment complex, I turned around to see the hundreds of units there—and it hit me, "Somebody is collecting and will deposit hundreds of checks just like mine." Then I realized they would deposit these checks this month and again next month and again the next! A money machine, the owners of that apartment complex owned a money machine!

I didn't take any action at that time, but it was something I began to ponder. I really didn't know how to start or what to do, and as a college student I didn't have any money anyway. I graduated with nothing but a degree and student loan debt.

After graduation, I took a job that I hated making a salary that just barely covered the bills. I never forgot my aha moment from the apartment complex though I still didn't act on it. Frankly, I didn't know how to act on it or how to get started owning real estate.

After renting a house another year after college, I decided I should at least buy my first house. I thought about buying a duplex and renting one side of it. That way, the tenant next door to me would pay my mortgage for me. That might put me on the same track as the apartment owners. A grand idea, I thought!

But, for some reason, I didn't do it. I bought a single-family house. So, guess who paid the mortgage? I did! I paid it out of my not-so-great salary that previously I'd been paying rent from. It would have been nice to have had tenants on one side of a duplex covering my payment or at least a large portion of it. That would have been a smarter thing to do from an investment perspective. I could have saved more money and begun to generate a small amount of passive income!

So, owning didn't really feel a lot different from renting, except for the fact that it was mine. I had some pride of ownership knowing that I owned my own place. I remember at the closing table being scared to death when I signed the mortgage papers promising to make a payment to the bank every month for the next 30 years to pay back the $100K I'd just borrowed to make the purchase. But, it was my first step. And after buying that one to live in, it was easier to buy the next one and easier to buy rental properties. Since that day, I've personally bought a number of houses and worked directly or indirectly with clients to buy lots of houses, which I'll detail to you later in this chapter.

I got married shortly after buying that first house, and my wife and I lived there for about four years. Because we decided to upgrade and buy a larger home before starting our family, we sold that house. I made about $10,000 on the sale. At the time, I thought I had made great money! However, looking back, keeping that house to rent out would have been really smart. Sure, I made money when I sold it, which at that time was big money for me, but I still regret selling it.

Looking back, I should have kept it. That house would most likely now rent for around $1,300 per month. My payment was only $600 per month, so I could be making $700 per month (or $8,400 per year) on it if I still owned it. So, I would be making almost as much EVERY year as I made during that one sale. That purchase did very little to move me toward owning rental property, building monthly cash flow, and achieving financial freedom.

Slow, Risky & Cumbersome: The Traditional Route

All of this was during the early years of our marriage before we had children. It wasn't until later that I really began to see real estate as a viable retirement vehicle. All my life I'd been told to put away part of my paycheck into my employer's 401K and to invest in IRAs every year. I'd been taught about the benefits of a ROTH IRA and taught to steadily invest and to diversify among stocks and mutual funds. My wife and I both put small portions of our paychecks into our employers' matching 401K plans. I also had a financial advisor that I met with occasionally for future planning.

I learned that to figure out how much I would need to save for retirement, I needed to figure out when I wanted to retire, how long I thought I would live after I retired, and how much money I would need to live on and pay my bills in retirement. That's enough to make my head spin! That's a lot to figure out with a lot of unknowns a long time into the future. It seemed like chasing a moving target. Not having any clarity and not being able to see a clear path just didn't seem like a good idea.

Ideally, you would want to save enough money for retirement that you could live off of the growth and interest of that retirement account each year. If you start pulling out principal, then your returns will decrease each year. If you are healthy and live a long life, you run a high risk of outliving your retirement.

So how much would you need to save in a traditional retirement account to replace your income? Vanguard has an online calculator that I found. I don't know how accurate it is, but I ran these calculations, assuming you begin investing at age 30 and retire at age 65. This means you are saving money for 35 years.

If you get returns of 8%, you need to save 28% of your income each year in order to have the same paycheck you have while you are working. These percentages apply regardless of your income. For the examples, I used $5,000 per month, or $60K per year. In order to match that same income when you retire, you need to save $16,500 per year, which is about $1,400 per month for 35 years! That's to have $5000 per month when you retire.

If you can consistently get a return of 10%, you'll need to save 18% of your income or $900 every single month for 35 years ($11,000 per year).

At a 6% return, you would need to save almost 42% of your income or $25K of your $60K salary each year for 35 years!

Stop reading for a moment and plug your own figures into the calculation at the website below:

https://RetirementPlans.Vanguard.com/VGApp/pe/pubeducation/calculators/RetirementIncomeCalc.jsf

If for some reason the website link above isn't working, then do a search of the following words to find it: "Vanguard retirement income calculator."

In a nutshell, according to Vanguard, you need to be saving 18% to 42% of your income each year, depending on the return you are going to get, in order to replace the income you currently have unless you have other investments or income streams you can depend on. These calculations also do not factor in social security. Frankly, I just don't know how reliable that source will be either in future years.

Honestly, this calculator doesn't even really make sense to me. When I do simple math, and assume I save $25K per year for 35 years, that equals $875K without any interest during the 35 years. Just straight math. At a 6% return, it would equal $52,500 per year that could be drawn. They are calculating 3% for inflation, but it's still difficult to understand. This is coming from the money managers, so I can only assume it's accurate. But again, it's confusing and difficult to figure out just how much you really need to be saving.

The takeaway: real estate is much simpler, and I'll show you why—and how—throughout this book. But first we'll continue to consider the traditional way.

In order to calculate how much you need to be saving each month, you need to know what your return will be. So, what kind of return is realistic? Will you get 6% return or 8% return? Who knows with the stock market? It has had years of boom and years of bust. You can be doing great one year and then lose 20% to 30% in a year. I'm not sure why, but the Vanguard calculator does not allow the user to plug in a return beyond 10%. I think it's because they don't expect a return higher than 10% on average for the long term. Several sources indicate the S&P 500 has gained around 7% on average for the past 20 years. Who knows if the next 20 years will be more or less?

The following chart[1] shows the S&P 500 returns each year over the past 20 years.

S&P 500 ANNUAL RETURNS

Year	Return	Year	Return	Year	Return	Year	Return
1998	26.67%	2003	26.38%	2008	-38.49%	2013	29.60%
1999	19.53%	2004	8.99%	2009	23.45%	2014	11.39%
2000	-10.14%	2005	3.00%	2010	12.78%	2015	-0.73%
2001	-13.04%	2006	13.62%	2011	0.00%	2016	9.54%
2002	-23.37%	2007	3.53%	2012	13.41%	2017	19.42%

The returns have soared in some years and tanked in others. My problem with this is that it's simply unpredictable. What if you were planning to stop working and retire at the end of 2002? You would have lost 46% of your portfolio in the past 3 years! You would have to continue working and eventually gain it back in 2006. But what if you then decided to work a little longer until the end of 2008 since things were looking better? Then you would have lost over 38% in that one year! Ouch!

My point to all of this—how can anyone really know how well their stocks will perform or how much they will really need to save to be ready for retirement?

According to the AARP, a couple will have needed to save $1.18 million when they retire in order to have a $40K income each year and that would last them for 30 years after retirement.[2]

Can you save $1.18 million? If you can save $1.18M, can you live off of $40K in retirement? According to CNN Money, most Americans are spending more than $40K in retirement.[3] I understand that some believe that retirees don't need the same amount of money they did when they were working because they will have less expenses. I don't buy that. How will their expenses be less? Because they get the senior discount at Denny's? I think not! I think expenses will be the same or more. Using this same principle, to have $80K income, you would need to save twice as much, or $2.36M. If you make $80K per year now and want to continue your lifestyle in retirement, is it realistic to think you can save $2.36M between now and then? How?

Several sources online indicate that healthcare costs are rising, and many estimate healthcare costs to be $200K to $275K out of pocket in retirement.[4,5] I also don't think that most predictions take into account leisure and travel during their retirement years. How boring would it be to retire and just sit at home watching *Wheel of Fortune* and watering your flowers? That's not the kind of retirement that I want.

Personally, I want to continue living in retirement! If I'm going to be healthy and live to be 95, I want to be traveling, going to the beach and lake, spending time with family, volunteering and doing mission work, and enjoying life during those early retirement years. Honestly, I'm so driven I may never really truly retire in the sense that I stop working. I can't sit still, so I'll be doing something. But, I don't want to have to rely on working for an income. I want a passive income, so that I'm free to do whatever I choose to do later in life. Don't you?

One of the problems with traditional retirement planning is that most Americans are living paycheck-to-paycheck and simply aren't saving at all for retirement. And when they see the huge amounts they'll need to be storing away to lead to anything substantial in retirement, it just doesn't seem realistic. It's discouraging. There has to be a better way.

There is a better way—and that's what I'll be showing you in this book!

Another problem is that for most, as their income rises, their spending adjusts to absorb the additional amount of money they are making. We'll discuss this more in future chapters, but do all you can to keep your expenses low, even when your income rises. Then you can put that additional income to work for you and your future. And whether you choose the traditional stock-investing route for retirement or the real estate route, you'll need funds to do it. This book will show you how you can do it much more easily and quickly and with less of your own money through real estate.

Most Americans don't have enough money saved for retirement and many will struggle. Social Security benefits will be questionable in coming years, especially for younger generations. Those funds are likely to run out in my opinion.

However, let's say you are a saver and you can save $900 to $2100 per month as the Vanguard site recommends in order to have $60K per year income. This is an estimated $11,000 to $25,000 per year in savings. If you can do this, then I can show you how you can replace your income much more quickly than 35 years with income-producing real estate. This book will teach you how to do it in less than half the time. Or if you invest at this rate in the right real estate for 35 years, you'll see how you can have an exponentially higher income and a much better retirement than you would if investing in traditional stocks and bonds.

If you can't save this amount, real estate may still be a viable option for you. It will take you longer to replace your income, but it's still much better than stocks and bonds, and will result in you having a much more lucrative retirement. It is a better path than traditional stocks, bonds, mutual funds, and IRAs.

So, you have the option of sticking with traditional means of saving for retirement, which, in my opinion, does more to help the financial managers make commissions than helping you be ready for retirement. Or you can look for a new vehicle. That new vehicle is income-producing rental property! It's reaps returns for you faster, requires you to invest less of your own money, and, based on my experience, is more secure.

MORE SIMPLE, MORE CERTAIN, MORE REASONABLE: THE REAL ESTATE WAY

After seeing what would be required of us to save for retirement the traditional way and comparing that to investing in real estate, I quickly and easily chose my path. I became a real estate agent in 2004 and began to get an inside look at how others were creating financial freedom for themselves in their 30s and 40s. They didn't have to wait until they are 65 to retire. Most are still working because they want to.

Around this time, I also read Robert Kiyosaki's *Rich Dad, Poor Dad*, and that book changed my thinking. In it, Kiyosaki compares the differences in how his "two dads" (one who was actually his best friend's dad) thought about and acted with money. While both made a good income, one constantly struggled with money while the other grew wealthy. If you haven't read it, I highly recommend it.

The inside look at real estate investors that I personally met, combined with what I learned from *Rich Dad, Poor Dad,* acted as huge eye-openers for me. Suddenly, I could see the incredible possibilities of income-producing real estate, and the freedom it could create. And now, I've experienced it personally.

You don't have to become a real estate agent in order to make real estate investments work for you. You can continue in your current job and simply have a real estate agent help you find and purchase the investment properties. I just happened to change careers because I hated my previous job and it helped me get an inside look at the possibilities.

I like to think that I'm smarter now and that I manage money and assets more wisely. Since buying that first house, I've bought and sold several. Some homes I've bought and kept as rental properties. Others I've flipped for a quick profit and used those profits to buy and hold other properties. In fact, I've invested in enough properties that I now receive a sizeable annual income from my real estate investments. However, I won't consider myself officially free until the debt is paid off on all of these properties, which is what I'm working toward now. Proverbs 22:7 states, "The borrower is slave to the lender." Since my goal is complete freedom in life, I've got to get the debt paid off. In addition, once the debt payments are gone, my net income will rise even more because the payments are gone. This kind of knowledge and financial freedom is what I want for you too, and it's what I lay out for you in this book.

The only regret I have at this stage in my life is not buying more houses to rent and not buying more of them when I was younger. The houses I bought 13 to 15 years ago are now paid down to almost half of what I originally paid, and they are worth quite a bit more than what I paid for them. And, technically, tenants made those monthly payments, not me. Of course, I made them, but I did it with monthly rent payments received from someone else. It's incredible really. The bank loaned me most of the money that I've used to purchase these properties, and complete strangers, the tenants, have given me the money each month to pay back the bank, plus extra money each month. They get up every morning and go to work, so they can send me a monthly check that I use to buy an asset for myself and my family. The property is in my name, and I own it while its equity (equity refers to the difference between a home's value and the amount of debt on it) is rising, yet the tenants provide the funds to pay for it. I can choose to sell the properties or continue to rent them and reap the benefits. To top it off, the rents have increased significantly over the past 10 years. When equity grows and rents increase, the magic really starts to happen!

REAL ESTATE:
THE BEST INVESTMENT FOR THE LONG TERM

I personally believe that almost everyone should have real estate for at least a portion of their investment and retirement strategy. For some people, it's just not right for them, and we'll discuss that in the next chapter. But, if you are reading this, you are intrigued by the idea, so it should be something you consider. Personally, I have very little stock, no 401K, and no commodities. I don't actively invest in stocks, bonds, currencies, or commodities. My retirement plan is real estate. Plain and simple.

After just 15 years of investing in real estate, I'm already producing more passive income from it than the average salary. I don't say this to boast or to brag. Deuteronomy 8:18 states that it is God who gives us the power to gain wealth, so I fully acknowledge that all I have comes from Him. Without Him giving me the knowledge and ability to do what I do, I would have nothing. Even the air I breathe comes from Him. So, I'm not boasting about what I've done. I'm only illustrating it to show you that you can do it too if you follow the instructions in this book. I feel it is my duty to help others with the knowledge I have been given.

So, what makes real estate such a great investment?

Several reasons. All of these may or may not apply in your situation, and we'll go into these deeper later in this book, but consider the following:

1. *It's real.* It's a piece of the earth. In my opinion, real estate is simply a better investment because it's real. You can see it, touch it, smell it, walk on it. And you have more control over its performance because you own it. You can't do anything to control whether a stock price goes up or down unless you have a majority ownership in the company.

2. *It's secure.* Specifically, residential real estate because people always need a place to live. Providing a place for your family to stay warm in winter, cool in summer, and dry in the rain is more important than automobiles, vacations, etc. Housing is a necessity. In fact, it's the second tier on Maslow's hierarchy of needs,[6] and it comes right after the basic need of food. If the economy gets really bad, people will pay for housing before they pay for other things.

3. *It's stable.* In a down economy, the value of real estate may go down. Stocks and other assets will also go down in a bad economy. However, the real estate will always be there and will always provide value to whoever is living in it. It will still produce rental income. Stocks can literally go to zero.

4. You don't have to sell real estate to get paid. Unless a stock pays a dividend, and many don't, you must sell shares to get cash. If a stock does pay a dividend, it's usually a small one. Real estate pumps out cash every month without you having to sell it. You keep the asset that over time goes up in value, and it still pays you every single month.

5. It provides you leverage. Will your bank give you a loan for 80% of your stock purchase? No. They will with real estate. And with leverage, if done properly, the tenant actually covers the mortgage with their monthly rent payment, and you STILL collect cash each month. This allows you to build momentum and grow your portfolio on your way to retirement.

6. Tax benefits. You can depreciate real estate (take tax deductions) while it appreciates (goes up) in value. The interest if you have a mortgage is also tax deductible. Chapter 10 addresses these tax advantages in more detail.

7. It is very forgiving. I've made mistakes and seen others make mistakes in real estate, but because of the investment itself, it's easier to be creative and find a way to make the investment work rather than losing it all. A stock can literally go to zero if the company you are investing in goes under. It's not likely for real estate to go to zero.

8. More people are renting. This trend means a higher demand for rental units. Even more seniors are now choosing to rent. Since 2006, the number of homeowners in the US has declined and the number of renters has increased.[7]

9. My favorite reason—monthly CASH FLOW.

I get paid passive income every single month from the properties I own. I don't have to wait for the values to up in order to make money.

Reaping Big

Most people who are homeowners would agree that their house has been their "best investment." Or at least one of their best investments. You hear it all the time. If one house is their best investment, what would multiple houses mean? Wouldn't it be wise to own more than one?

A home is a tax shelter and a forced savings account for most Americans. What I mean by that is that each month as you pay that mortgage, the balance gets smaller and smaller, building what is called equity. Over time, the equity grows and eventually, once the loan is paid off, the owner's equity is the full value of the home. To repeat, equity is defined as the difference between the value of a home and the amount of debt on it. For example, if you own a home that's worth $200K, and you have a loan of $150K, then you have $50K equity in the home. If you sold it and paid off the mortgage, you are left with the equity of $50K, which can be converted to cash. Over time as you pay down that $150K mortgage, the debt gets smaller and the equity gets larger. Additionally, if the home appreciates in value, then the homeowner's equity grows as well. With rental property, it's not even the owner who pays off the loan. The tenant pays it off with rent payments made to the owner. So, when I say it's wise to own more than one home, I don't mean a vacation home or second home. I mean an income-producing property that someone else pays for because it provides them a place to live.

While cars, clothing, food, and everything else that's real have gone up in price over the years, so has real estate. Yes, we did have a recession recently, but the only people that lost in real estate during that recession are the people who sold their homes for less than they paid or those who let their homes go back to the bank. No one else lost money. And now, 2018, generally home values are higher than they were pre-recession.

As a real estate agent, I helped several buyers, many who were first-time homebuyers, to purchase homes during the recession. They were buying them for literally half of their pre-recession value. Now, many have sold and doubled their money. It's nice to see young couples sell their homes and walk away with $50K to $100K tax-free. It's because they bought real estate. Those who rented a place to live for the past 10 to 15 years don't have that opportunity.

Investors have also sold homes they bought during those time periods and made a lot of money. For the investors, the payments were covered by the tenants, but they can now sell for large profits. Just imagine what it's like for those who bought 10, 20, or even hundreds of homes during the downturn. There are those who did it, and they are reaping big benefits now.

Personally, I bought a few houses prior to the recession. When the values plummeted, I wondered if I had made a mistake. However, I held on, let the tenants continue to make the payments, and I've got great equity in those homes now. Even if the equity didn't come back, those houses continue to pay me every single month. And they paid me every month during the recession. I would have lost if I had lost sight of my long-term vision, became fearful, and sold when prices were low. Actually, I was able to refinance those mortgages to shorter terms, lower interest rates, and lower payments during the recession.

I wish I had bought homes in 2010 and 2011 when prices were at the bottom. Hindsight being 20/20, I would be in a much better financial situation now. I was actually digging into savings just to pay bills during those years. There was no commission money left over to invest in real estate even though it was the best time in decades to buy. If I had known more about the alternative funding strategies discussed in Chapter 8 at that time, I would likely own more houses now.

My income was actually negative in 2010. That's right, the income on my tax return was a negative number, meaning it went backwards for that year. My business expenses were higher than the income I received. However, now, less than 10 years later, I am earning more than an average salary through passive income-producing real estate. When done properly, income-producing real estate is a powerful wealth builder and monthly cash-flow builder.

If you have money sitting in the stock market, a savings account, or CDs, and you are not happy with the performance, consider moving some or all of it to real estate. Even if you are happy with your returns, consider diversifying it. At the time of this writing in 2018, the stock market is soaring. However, we could see a correction at any time. What would happen if you saw the stock market adjust downward 30% to 35% over the next year? How would that affect your net worth and your retirement plans?

I think you'll find that, when done correctly, your real estate investment(s) will outperform most other simple investment vehicles. To find out how, continue reading.

CHAPTER 2
Is Real Estate Right for You?

You must decide if investing in real estate is right for you and your personal situation. We are going to get into the pros and cons throughout this book. As you go through it, either you'll get really excited about real estate or you won't. If you do, real estate may be for you. If you don't, quite honestly, you might want to find another investment vehicle. In my opinion, income-producing real estate is a better investment than most other options, but if you aren't excited about it, don't do it. While it's a mostly passive investment, it will require some action on your part and you'll need to be willing to take that action, which we'll review in the coming chapters.

Owning rental property is not for everyone. In this chapter, I'm going to outline the aspects that some people find difficult. I'm not sharing this with you to scare you. I simply want you to have a good idea of what you're getting into and show you the full picture.

EYES WIDE OPEN: THE RISKS

There are risks involved. These risks are numerous. These risks include things like making unexpected repairs, making mortgage payments, and dealing with tenants.

Homes and their systems are man-made and mechanical, so things will fail. Homes must be maintained, or they will deteriorate and cost more money to repair later. You must be able to make decisions about caring for the properties. And you must have the cash on hand to make these repairs when they are necessary.

If you purchase with financing, then you must make a monthly mortgage payment even when the property is vacant. If you don't make that payment, you'll lose the property in foreclosure. You are exposed to the volatility of the market. If the market goes down, can you handle it? I don't expect real estate values to fall again like they did during the Great Recession. However, no one knows. It could happen again. It's bad enough to see one property you own go down 40%. What if you own multiple properties, and all of their values go down 40%? Losing 40% on ten homes is worse than losing 40% on one. Again, this is only a paper loss unless you sell. But, it's a loss in your mind, your balance sheet, and a loss to your financial net worth either way. If you have loans, the banks could ask for more cash, depending on your loan structure. If you are going to invest in real estate, you must have the guts and the will to get through these tough times without losing your sanity.

There are people involved when it comes to owning real estate. These people include tenants who must be handled and dealt with properly. Some of the situations with tenants can be very uncomfortable. Can you handle it when they have a pet they aren't supposed to have? Can you have the hard conversation when they don't pay the rent? Do you have the backbone to evict them when necessary? You must be willing to treat real estate investing as a business because that's what it is.

Will you be able to handle repairs that are needed from time to time like leaky faucets, replacing a ceiling fan, or repairing a heating and air unit? On that rare occasion, when a tenant moves out and the walls are busted up and the carpet is stained and smells like pet urine, are you going to keep a level head? Are you going to be able to restore the property, put it back in service, and keep going? Or, will you be too upset to even function? Some people are too upset and simply can't handle it mentally. I've worked with these kinds of clients, and they end up making irrational and emotional decisions that aren't good for them. It causes them to make mistakes. You have to go into it realizing that these kinds of things happen occasionally and are just part of the business. A myth is that tenants always leave houses completely trashed and in disrepair, but reality is they rarely do. As you gain experience or have an experienced manager, you can greatly minimize these kinds of events.

Some landlords don't know how to handle tenants and repairs, and these are the ones who complain about owning real estate. These are the ones that will tell you it's a bad investment and to stay away from it. Not managing the property and the tenants properly can be the difference in making a great profit from owning real estate and losing it all.

You need to make sure that owning real estate is something you want to do. Some owners get around these issues by hiring professional management. This way, they don't have to deal with the tenants or the repairs or damages. They simply see the financial side of it and entrust the management of the property and tenants to someone else.

By hiring a top-notch property management firm, a lot of these headaches are removed from you. While you are still involved to a degree, it makes it a more "passive" investment, like your stock portfolio. And honestly, if you are a busy individual, who owns a business, works a lot of hours, has a family, or generally does not have a lot of free time, I definitely recommend you turn your property over to a management company. We'll talk more about finding and hiring a property manager later in chapters 11 and 12.

Unless you have plenty of time and enjoy the tedious tasks that come along with owning and leasing property, hiring a manager is what you need to do. Relatively speaking, property management is cheap compared to the value you will get from it. Even with professional property management, you must be prepared for expenses to arise related to owning the property. This should be expected and not surprise you. Owning rental real estate can be messy, but it can be lucrative.

So, if you don't think you can mentally handle dealing with expenses and tenants, then you may want to avoid investing in real estate. If you can't do it yourself or trust a property manager to handle things for you, then it may not be for you. However, if you are able to see the big picture, understand how lucrative owning rental property can be, and navigate the challenges of it, then keep reading because this book is for you.

Besides making sure you can face the not-so-easy part of owning real estate, you need to make sure you are prepared financially. That's what the next chapter is all about.

CHAPTER 3
The Financial Prerequisites

If you aren't in the right place with your finances, you can fail before you even get started. I strongly recommend you take the advice of this chapter before you buy your first property.

Before you can begin buying real estate, you need to make sure your personal finances are in order. If you have loads of cash, then this chapter may not apply to you. But, if you are trying to buy your first rental house, you need to consider these four prerequisites.

One—if you are living paycheck-to-paycheck and spending 100% of what you make every month, in my opinion, you are not ready to buy rental property. You need to either find a way to increase your income or reduce your monthly expenses.

Two—if you have credit card debt or other consumer debt, in my opinion, you need to eliminate those before investing in real estate. The more you can eliminate other debt, the faster you will get to your goal of being financially free, and the funds that are currently going toward those payments can be put toward your investing. Also, as you pay off this consumer debt, your credit score will be higher, which will enable you to get a loan from the bank more easily and with better terms.

Three—you need to have some funds set aside to cover unexpected property repairs or surprises as they come along. So, in addition to your down payment for the property, or the purchase price if you are paying cash, you need to have some funds set aside in case you need to replace a heating and air unit, water heater, roof, etc. Repairs can often be unexpected, so make sure you have a back-up plan. The back-up plan is funds set aside ONLY for unexpected surprises like major repairs or vacancies.

Four—if you are planning to finance the purchase with a traditional bank, you'll need a minimum of 20% as your down payment. There will also be loan and closing fees that will typically be in the range of 3% to 5% for the average property. If you are paying cash, your closing fees will be less, but you'll need 100% of the purchase price.

In chapters 7 and 8, we'll discuss options for buying homes without a down payment. It's more difficult, but there are ways to do it. However, in my opinion, you'll be in a much better position to be successful in the long run if you start with some money in the bank.

Why these four prerequisites? While it's not imperative that you have 20% cash on hand, I still recommend minimizing your other expenses and ridding yourself of consumer debt before buying real estate. Otherwise, it will add a ton of additional stress and you're setting yourself up for failure if even one little thing goes wrong. If you have too much money going out each month and not enough coming in, you will not be prepared to weather the storms as they come.

So, if you already have at least 20% of the purchase price to put down, funds for reserve, and have no consumer debt, you can move to the next chapter, although reading to the end of this chapter may give you some additional insights and ideas. If you are not financially prepared, read on and focus on getting yourself ready to become a real estate investor and find your financial freedom.

Not Quite There Yet?

If you currently are living paycheck-to-paycheck and struggling just to pay bills, I understand. I've been there. But, you absolutely cannot remain in this place. It's imperative that you figure out ways to cut your expenses and increase your income, so you can invest. A small amount of discipline in this area now will reward you handsomely in years to come. You must commit to it. You must have the willpower and self-discipline to make changes.

This may seem like a huge obstacle to get to a place where all of your consumer debts are gone, you have a reserve account, and you have 20% down. It seemed like a big step to me as well before I bought my first rental house. Remember, you've got to start somewhere and once you start, you'll have more income, which will pay down more debt, which will increase your income. It's a snowball effect once you get going. But, you must start.

To start, you've got to have the discipline, hustle, and desire to make it happen. So, how do you get to a place you can start?

Spend Less

The first step is to begin living below your means. In simple terms, you need to spend less than you make. And if you are carrying a credit card balance right now, then either you are not living below your means or you have not lived below your means in the past. You must pay more than the monthly minimum on those cards, and you must stop adding new charges. Cut up those cards or lock them away.

There are only two ways to get ahead financially. One way is to cut expenses. The other way is to increase income. That's it. Only two ways!

My preferred method is to increase income. That's proven to be a better path for me. It's easier for some than it is for others, but you must do one or, even better, a combination of both cutting expenses and raising income at the same time!

A BUDGET

Create a budget. Go through all of your expenses and see where you can cut out some unnecessary expenditures. Can you do without cable TV with the extra sports package, eat out less, or take a cheaper vacation? Stop spending your money on unnecessary things. Find out where you can make cuts and make them. Be disciplined enough now so that you can reap the rewards later. It's called delayed gratification. The more you can delay now, the more you can be grateful for later.

DISCIPLINE OR REGRET: YOUR CHOICE

I'm reminded of a study I read about regarding kids and delayed gratification.[8] The study was conducted by a psychologist with a major university decades ago. Children were placed in a room and given the choice of having one treat now, a marshmallow, cookie, etc., or they had a second option that would reap them more rewards: not eat the treat immediately, and instead wait for a few minutes to receive two treats. The follow-up study proved that the children who could exercise the willpower, self-discipline, and delayed gratification to wait a few minutes to get two treats proved to be more successful in testing and generally more successful later in life.

This self-discipline will translate to all areas of life, not just finances. It takes self-discipline to stay healthy, to eat right, and to exercise. It takes self-discipline to learn a new skill. Those who can exercise proper self-discipline and willpower can get ahead.

The late Jim Rohn, one of my favorite motivational speakers, said, "We must all suffer from one of two pains: the pain of discipline or the pain of regret. The difference is discipline weighs ounces while regret weighs tons."

So, you can either exercise discipline and willpower now to have a better future, or you can regret not having the discipline when you are actually in the future and can't afford to take care of yourself.

I encourage you to stop reading right now, sit down, go through your bank account, and itemize all of your expenditures for the past month. Then go through with a different colored pen and start marking which ones you could have done without. Then total that figure. That's how much you could save each month. Use that amount to start paying off your consumer debts and getting your finances in order for a better future.

I can guarantee you that there is someone, somewhere, living on less income than you are. They may not be as comfortable as you are, but they are doing it nonetheless.

The more you can cut from your expense column, the faster you can get to your financial goals. If you can only cut a small amount, that's OK. It just might take you longer to get there unless you are able to increase your income.

Dave Ramsey, businessman and author, likes to say, "Live life now like no one else, so you can live later like no one else." What he means is live without as much now, so you can be wealthy and live better than everyone else later. And by the way, he has some great resources about getting out of debt, creating a budget, etc. Let me add that while he gives great advice and I follow many of his teachings, I don't agree with him 100% on everything he says. For example, he is very anti-debt. I believe there is good debt and bad debt, and I think debt has its place and can be used as a tool. (We'll discuss this more later as well.) Debt is often misused, and that's when people get into trouble. So, while I follow his teachings and agree with him on most points, I don't agree with him on every point. That's OK. His ideas have helped me a lot, and he makes a lot of sense. So, read his books or take his courses. You may find some insight as well.

More Cost-Cutting Ideas

If you have credit cards, cut them up or put them where you no longer have access to them. If the numbers are saved on your favorite websites, delete them out. If you have an automobile and you are making payments, you might consider selling it and buying an older, but well-maintained used car for cash, so you eliminate that payment. Find ways to free up cash each month so that you can knock out the debt and save for your down payment and future investing.

While cutting expenses is one method, it's hard! It's really hard! And, you have to make a lot of cuts and a lot of sacrifices to save a little bit of money. And it takes a long time of saving just a little bit of money to add up to enough to put 20% down on a property.

If you make $60K per year, and you are able to cut expenses by 10%, that's $6,000. That's a lot of money, but at that pace, it will take a few years for you to save enough for a down payment. But, if you remember from the previous chapter about saving for retirement, you need to be putting this money away and investing it somewhere anyway to secure your future.

I really think this is the main reason people give up and don't even try to invest. They throw their hands up and decide it's just not worth it.

They aren't committed for the long haul, and they lose sight of their future. They would rather live paycheck-to-paycheck and figure out their future later. But really that's like sticking your head in the sand and pretending it doesn't matter. It does matter. I know it's hard to do without things you like when you see others having them. I get it. And there is an alternative to pinching every penny. It takes a lot of work too, but it is my preferred method.

UPPING YOUR INCOME

My preferred method is to increase income. I've found that if you are creative and work hard, it can be easier to increase income than it is to cut expenses. If you work an hourly or salaried job, it's not going to be easy for you to increase your income because you are not in control of it. However, I've seen employees who work really hard move up the ranks and see rapid rises in income. This happens when they are working for an employer who really sees what they are contributing and appreciates it.

Well-Compensated for Your Worth—if you are providing lots of value for the company you work for, they should see it and reward you for it. If not, go provide the value to another company that will appreciate you or go create your own way by working for yourself. If you feel you are really contributing to your company and not being paid what you are worth, go ask for a raise!

The only way you can have complete control of your income is to become self-employed, build a business, or find a commission sales job. Improve your skills and go make more money! Find something you can excel at where your income is not capped.

Side Hustle—another option would be to create a side hustle where you are selling a product or service either online or through multilevel marketing or something of that sort. I'm not a huge fan of multilevel marketing, but I've seen people do really well with the right product, the right team, and the right support.

If you can't bear the thought of working for yourself, you might just consider a part-time job working for someone else and then pay off debt or save all of the money you earn from the extra job. You will have a guaranteed income this way, and it will be steady. There is less risk this way. However, when working for yourself, if you are successful, you can move the needle much faster.

Second Income—if your spouse doesn't work, let your spouse get a job and earn the extra income. Then all of this new income can go toward investing or getting yourself prepared to invest.

Invest One Salary—in fact, if you are newly married, I recommend you start out learning to live off of one income. If you are single and not yet married, but plan to be in the future, let that be a goal. Live off only one income even after you get married and you are both earning incomes. That will put you and your new spouse years ahead of your peers when it comes to investing and getting ahead. You can save and invest one salary every year!

When my wife and I were first married, she had a part-time job and I had the full-time job, so we learned to live on less. Once she got hired full-time (and was actually making more than me), we continued to live off of the same income, which allowed us to completely save almost all of what she made. Do you think that made it easier for us to get started investing? Yes, it did!

Play Defense—a mistake that most people make is as they begin making more money or as they get a higher paying job, they immediately find something to spend the extra income on. They either buy a new house to live in, a new car, new boat, new clothes, or something. And within a few months they are back to living paycheck-to-paycheck. This is a huge mistake. So, when you get that extra job, that raise, or you start making money from a side hustle, don't spend it! Don't earn extra income in order to spend more. **Earn more, so you can invest more!**

Figure out how to increase your income but continue to live off of the same amount. This is what I call playing defense. It allows you to keep some funds to invest in assets that will produce income back to you.

The average salary in the US is $81,400 per year. So, if you can live off that and your spouse also makes $80K per year, then you can get out of debt and get started buying investment property fast! The problem for most people is that if the household income is $160K, they spend $160K, or sometimes even $170K, every year. If you can learn to live off of one income, then you can really make huge strides with your investments and replace that income very quickly.

In Georgia, where I live and work, the average income is $59,100. How different could things be if you could save that amount of money each year to invest?

A Caveat

I also want to give you one word of caution. While having money to invest is important, keeping your family together and spending time with your spouse and your children is even more important. So, before you go get a second job or your spouse gets another job, weigh the cost and make sure you are not sacrificing your family for a dollar. If you strongly believe that one spouse needs to be home with young children, then don't sacrifice that conviction in order to gain financially. Your family and children will always be more important than finances.

Please read that previous paragraph again. Do not sacrifice your family just so you can get ahead financially. If you have millions and millions of dollars, but no family to spend it with, what have you gained? In my opinion, you lose.

GOOD VS. BAD DEBT

Earlier, I mentioned good debt and bad debt. It's interesting, but in some cases, I can agree with using debt; in the other cases, I hate it.

I hate consumer debt. I hate credit card payments. I hate car payments. I just don't like having extra payments each month. They are such a burden and weigh heavy. And they come up every month. It's enough to pay for electricity, food, cell phones, Internet, entertainment, etc. I don't want to also pay a credit card, car payment, time-share payment, and boat payment too! It's just too much.

To look at the flip side of that coin, I like recurring money coming in every month (in the form of rent), but I don't like it going out every month in the form of payments. If you can flip the equation, so you have more and more people paying you each month and you are paying fewer and fewer bills each month, you are on the right track. I hope this is a light bulb moment for you.

Change your thinking and think of it this way: money is always flowing one way or another. You need to figure out how to make more of it flow into your account than flows out of your account. As more money flows in and less money flows out, that margin will grow and your bank account will grow. As you have more money, it can be invested to multiply and create more. It's like your money having babies and making more money.

When it comes to borrowing money to buy a house or condo to rent to someone else, I like using debt. Why? Because I can increase my income. Even though I have a new payment, and more cash going out, I like it. Because if I buy a rental property, add a new mortgage and new payment as an expense, I know I'm also increasing the amount coming in in the form of rent. If I have a new mortgage payment of $800 per month, but a new income stream of $1,200 per month, I'm adding $400 per month to my account. This is unlike new car payment of $800 per month, which does not add to my income. It only subtracts $800 per month from my account. I only want to add an expense IF I can add more income at the same time. Make sense? That's what I call good debt.

Borrowing to buy rental properties gives me leverage to buy more properties, so that I'm technically not the one paying for that debt. Who is paying it? The tenant, of course.

Every day, that tenant wakes up, goes to work, and earns a paycheck so that they can send me a payment each month for providing them a place to live. This increases my income. When I receive their check, I make the mortgage payment and put the extra cash in the bank for repairs, surprise expenses, and save it up so that I can buy more property. When I do this, the amount that I owe to the bank decreases little by little. And after 180 or 360 months, depending on how it's financed, it's paid off. Does the tenant then have title to the property? No! I do! And it's been covered by usually several different tenants over the years.

Think about this.

Read this next paragraph and let it sink in:

To invest in real estate, you can get money from a bank to purchase it, then get money from someone else that you don't even know (the tenant) to pay back the bank, yet you get to own the property and enjoy the cash flow, appreciation, and tax benefits that come with owning it. What other investment offers this? The tenant contributes to your net worth and eventually pays off the property for you.

I know what you are thinking—*there are taxes, insurance, new roofs, new water heaters, and all kinds of expenses.* Of course, the popular statement, "I don't want tenants calling me in the middle of the night because their toilet is stopped up," stops many people from buying real estate. However, I've never had one of my tenants call me in the middle of the night for a stopped-up toilet. That's just an excuse people make. And as we'll discuss later, by hiring a property manager, you never meet or ever speak with the tenant about anything. You just collect their money.

Yes, there are expenses, but when structured properly, the tenant covers those too and there is still money left over each month. That's how you get to a place of financial freedom. And, after 30 years, the house is likely going to be worth more than twice it's purchase price, and you'll own it free and clear.

I currently own a property that is worth more than twice what I paid for it, and I've only owned it for 10 years. The mortgage is not paid off, but I have way more equity in it than what I owe. If I sold it now, I would put more money in my bank account than I originally paid for it.

So, yes, it's hard work to get into a position where you can make your first investment. But, it's totally worth it. Can you imagine how your life could look if you owned ten homes free and clear when you are ready to retire? Or twenty homes? Or fifty homes? Or hundreds?

I only mention the larger numbers because I want to show you that it's doable. However, for most, just having enough to cover expenses will be the goal. And to acquire 10 homes prior to retirement is not hard to do and that could be enough to give you a six-figure retirement income. To me, that sounds much better and much easier than trying to save and invest $2M to $3M out of your paycheck into stocks and mutual funds to achieve the same lifestyle in retirement.

I know owning multiple homes may seem like a hard concept for you to imagine. It was for me 10 to 15 years ago as well, but as I bought the first one, then the second one, then more and more, it became more of a reality. And because each property makes you money, every time you add another one, your income rises. Because you keep expenses low as your income rises, each new house gives you more funds to buy another house, which gives you more funds to buy another house.

In chapters 7 and 8, we'll discuss options for buying properties and how to get the funding. However, before you can get the funding to make a purchase, you need to get those four prerequisites out of the way. These include paying off consumer debt and having some money in the bank.

Once your finances are in order, you are ready to go shopping for a property. Real estate is real estate, but there are several different types of real estate and they are all different. Within the different types, there are different classes as well, so before you can go shopping, you must know what you are shopping for. In the next chapter, we'll discuss the different kinds of income-producing real estate and the pros and cons of each.

CHAPTER 4
Choosing Niches: Key to Riches

When someone thinks of investing in real estate, that could mean a lot of things. There are a lot of directions and a lot of different kinds of real estate that can be purchased. While the context of this book is written primarily for investing in single-family residential properties, which is my personal focus, I want you to have an understanding of the other niches as well. And the general principle of income-producing real estate applies to all different areas and niches, but the nuances of each are different.

In this chapter, we'll discuss some of the more common types of real estate and the pros and cons of investing in each. For example, owning a single-family home is very different than owning a retail shopping center, which is very different than owning a mobile home park. They can all produce cash flow and income but are all quite different. You'll need to learn about the various types and determine which is best for you.

This chapter discusses the following property types:

- Single-Family Homes

- Condos/Townhomes

- Mobile/Modular Homes

- Mobile Home Parks

- Small Multifamily Homes

- Large Multifamily Homes

- Student Housing

- Commercial Property

- Land

Then among these different niches and property types, there are asset classes A, B, C, and D, which is a grading system to help you niche down even further. We'll take a look at these asset classes in this chapter as well.

The first and most common property type we'll discuss is the single-family home. I personally own more of these than any other type, and right now it's my favorite.

SINGLE-FAMILY HOMES

To start, let me give you a general definition of a single-family home. When I say single-family home, I'm referring to a detached home that one family would live in. Typically, these homes have between two and four bedrooms and between one and three bathrooms. They would have some kind of yard, large or small, and would not be attached to other structures, which differentiates them from condos, apartments, or duplexes.

In my opinion, single-family homes are the easiest and least risky types of investments you can make. They are easy because they typically attract a high-quality tenant who has a steady job, is mature, and is willing and able to pay more in rent than the cost of an apartment or condo.

Another advantage is that the tenants typically stay in single-family homes longer than they do in apartments or condos. The transition, or "turn," between tenants can be costly. Turning entails getting a unit ready to lease after one tenant leaves and before the next one comes in. It includes painting, cleaning, replacing flooring, etc. You want to minimize this as much as possible, and my experience has been that a tenant will stay in a single-family home often longer than they will stay in an apartment or duplex. Single-family homes also rent more easily and quickly when compared to other classes of real estate, based on my experience.

I also believe that these are the easiest to sell if they are bought in the right locations and they are kept in good condition. Single-family homes have better odds of appreciating rapidly, which means rising in value. I rarely recommend selling unless you have a need to sell or if you desire to reinvest to buy other properties. However, if you find yourself in a situation where you must sell, the single-family homes that make great rentals are generally easy to sell. These are the homes that might be considered starter homes. They are easier to sell than luxury homes simply because they are affordable and typically in high demand. These homes can be sold to another investor or to someone to live in.

Typically, you'll get the highest price by selling to someone that wants to live in it. It may be a first-time homebuyer or an empty nester. Either way, your buyer pool is larger because you have options to sell to more than just other investors whereas most of the other types of real estate we'll discuss would most likely only be sold to investors.

When selling to a homeowner, just keep in mind that the home will need to be free of a lease, and sometimes that can be tricky. It takes some planning ahead to sell it for top dollar. It's not as easy as selling a stock or some other paper investment, but selling a moderately priced single-family home in a good location is typically not hard to do, especially when you hire a great real estate agent to help you.

CONDOS/TOWNHOMES

Condos and townhomes are typically attached units that are very similar to their neighboring units and located in a community with multiple units. Condos and townhomes are going to look very similar to apartments, but unlike apartments that all have one owner, condos and townhomes have individual ownership. The legal difference between a condo and townhome is that when you buy a townhome, you do actually own the earth beneath the townhome. With a condo, the legal description is basically the unit itself, or one way to think of it is you only own the air space within the unit. With a condo, the ground and the earth under the unit are owned by the condominium association. The condo and townhome associations will also have rules and by-laws that must be adhered to as an owner of a unit in the development.

I would consider condo/townhomes to be next of kin to single-family homes. However, condos and townhomes typically will lease for less than a similar single-family detached house in the same area. On the flip side, they can also be purchased for less, so your return on investment (ROI) on condos is similar to single-family detached.

One thing that is different with condos and townhomes is that they typically include a monthly homeowner's association (HOA) fee. So, this fee will need to be figured into your cash flow calculation when you are considering it as an investment. This fee covers amenities that may be on the property, such as a pool, fitness center, lawn maintenance, trash pick-up, etc. These things are also very attractive to some tenants, so keep that in mind if you decide to invest in condos.

Amenities, location, and updates to the kitchen and bathroom are the things that will attract tenants. If the property has desirable amenities, the unit will be more desirable to rent as well. The location may be more or less desirable depending on what's around it. And the updates could be things that make the unit more modern like granite countertops, stainless appliances, and modern floors.

Some other benefits to you as an owner of a townhome or condo is that there is no lawn care or exterior maintenance that you will be responsible for, as the HOA will cover it. Some owners love condos because they are largely maintenance-free and some see them as easier to own and manage.

They can sometimes be harder to resell. Because condos are so similar, they often have the same floor plan, bedroom count, and finishes, so there is very little differentiation between units. You are at the mercy of what other units are selling for because units typically sell closer in price to the other units in the development whereas single-family homes are more unique and can have differing features even within the same subdivision.

Mobile/Modular Homes

Mobile and modular homes are similar to single-family homes. However, whereas most single-family homes are going to be built on site and permanently attached to the land, mobile and modular homes are built in a factory and assembled or installed onto the property. Often, they are permanently attached to the land, but the defining difference is that they are not built on-site. Due to this fact, they can be purchased at lower costs but are also typically less desirable because they are cheaper to build and considered lower quality.

Mobile homes are more common in some areas of the country than in others. In some areas, they are very common and you see them throughout town while in other places, they are only found in rural areas or less desirable or high-crime areas. So, choosing whether or not to invest in mobile homes is very likely location-specific. You'll need to make this determination.

Some things to consider are the fact that mobile homes are not built the same way that other structures are built. Since they are built in a factory, often with sub-par materials, and then taken to a location and set up on blocks or a concrete foundation, they can be less desirable. The positive thing about mobile homes is that they can be purchased less expensively than a single-family home. And, if the mobile home is on a lot in the country or even in a subdivision, it offers a lot of the same draws as a single-family home but will likely rent for less per month. It can also be purchased for less.

Financing can sometimes be difficult with mobile homes. It's difficult to get a long-term fixed-rate loan on a mobile home like you can with houses or condos. The Federal Housing Administration (FHA) will finance them for owner occupants if they have the proper tie-downs and meet their specifications for a permanent foundation along with other engineering guidelines.

Mobile homes actually have titles like automobiles when they are first manufactured. The only way to get financing through the FHA is for this title to be retired, which means the mobile home is considered permanently attached to the land. This is a process that you must go through and is state-specific, so do your research before investing in mobile homes. The FHA only provides financing for owner occupants, so it's not an option for investors. The only option for investors to purchase is to pay cash or work with a local bank for a short-term loan. We'll discuss financing options in more detail in chapters 7 and 8.

Since mobile homes are more difficult to finance, even for owners, keep that in mind as part of your exit strategy. They can be more difficult to sell conventionally. Some investors love mobile homes because the investor owners will owner finance them or sell them under a lease/purchase or lease/option. Chapter 15 will cover this in more detail.

The important thing for you to know is that mobile homes are different, so you need to go deep on understanding them before you invest. They can be great moneymakers and produce a great monthly cash flow if you have the right strategy.

MOBILE HOME PARKS

While we are on the topic of mobile homes, I'll go ahead and mention mobile home parks. Mobile home parks are communities of several mobile homes where all of the land (and sometimes the mobile homes also) is owned by one individual or entity. These are very much a niche and something that I personally don't have a lot of experience with. However, I do know that these can also be very lucrative if you know what you are doing.

There are two ways to make money with a mobile home park. One is to lease the structure on the lot just like any other dwelling. The other is to only lease the lot or the land that the mobile home sits on.

By leasing only the lot, as the landlord, you are not responsible for any repairs to the mobile home. You don't even own the home itself. So, when the AC breaks or the water heater fails or the roof leaks, you don't get phone calls. It's the tenant's property, so it's on them to repair. By owning the lot, you just have to make sure utilities are there, either sewer or septic, and that water is available. This hands-off approach is attractive to some investors. It's similar to a ground lease, billboard lease, or cell-phone tower lease.

Another attractive method to homes in parks is the opportunity to owner finance them to the occupants. Rob Minton, a real estate guru in Ohio, makes a lot of money buying these homes cheaply with cash inside of various parks and owner financing them to the buyers. He gets paid every month with interest. They cash flow very well, and he has excellent returns. If you are interested in learning more about owner financing mobile homes, do an Internet search of Rob Minton. He has some excellent resources on the topic, and I consider him an expert in mobile home investing and owner financing.

It seems that counties and municipalities are allowing fewer mobile homes in today's world. So, long term, I don't know how viable the option of owning mobile home parks will be. On the flip side, as cities no longer allow new parks and mobile homes are not being allowed in some parts of town, it could drive even more demand to existing parks and make them even more lucrative and valuable. There will always be a need for affordable housing.

Again, this is a category that I have not personally been involved in, so I'm not able to give first-hand experience or opinions. However, you now have basic knowledge and can explore it if this option seems like a good one for you.

SMALL MULTIFAMILY HOMES

I refer to duplexes, triplexes, and quadraplexes as small multifamily homes. The reason I classify them this way is that you can actually obtain conventional financing for these types of properties just like a single-family home. If you were trying to buy a larger apartment complex, the financing is completely different.

A duplex is one structure with two living spaces. It could also be called a two-family home. A triplex has three living spaces, and a quadraplex has four living spaces. These living spaces are defined as a unit where a family could live privately that includes bedrooms, bathrooms, a living area, and a kitchen. Sometimes these units could be one story, two stories, or more, but they would be adjoined together and located on the same lot, which means the families that live in the structure would typically share the yard space and parking area. Depending on the design of the structure, it could be possible to create independent yard space for each unit, but typically it's shared.

Some investors love having two to four units within the same structure. They like the idea of having multiple units together because it can make repairs easier. For example, there is only one roof for two, three, or four units whereas owning multiple single-family homes, there would be multiple roofs. Also, there is only one lot to maintain, one tax bill, etc.

Another reason investors are drawn to this category is they feel it diversifies their risk to an extent. We all know there will be some vacancies throughout the life of a rental property. Some investors like to structure their financing so that if they have a vacancy, they still have rental income to cover a mortgage. For example, if they own a duplex, they structure financing so that one unit covers the payment and the other unit is the profit. So, if one tenant moves, the owner doesn't have to use the reserve account to pay the mortgage.

In actuality, this same structure can be set up for single-family homes, condos, or anything else. And when individual properties are managed properly, vacancies either don't exist or are very short. My experience has been that duplexes, especially in my area, rent for less and attract tenants that may not meet my qualifications. If you relax your qualifications, then you may find yourself with a tenant who is not paying their rent. Then you have an even bigger problem.

I've also discovered that sometimes these properties are in less desirable areas, which causes them to turn over more often as tenants seem to move around more, which will create more vacancies. I've owned duplexes in these areas, and while on paper the ROI initially seems to be higher, in the long run and in reality, it wasn't for me. I had too many expenses turning units and making repairs. These tenants didn't seem to care for the property in the same way that tenants who lease single-family homes do.

If you can find a small multifamily property in a nice area that will attract good tenants and get higher returns, this could be a great option.

LARGE MULTIFAMILY HOMES

This classification would include an apartment complex with double-digit to triple-digit units all located on the same piece of property. For example, it may include 10 units, or there could be 950 units or more. If you are a beginner investor, then investing in a large multifamily is not going to be something that you would do. Even within the large multifamily category, there is a big difference between a 12-unit apartment building and a 500-unit apartment complex.

For our purposes, we'll lump them together, but in reality, they are vastly different. The ability to scale with larger developments is different than with smaller developments, and even your exit strategy is different. Generally, buyers who would be interested in a 500-unit community would not even consider looking at a 12-unit community. These larger investors are looking for scale.

It's possible that you could bring on a partner or buy into a syndication or something like that if you want to get into owning large apartment buildings. Since large multifamily is so much more complex, it's beyond the scope of this book, so I won't include a lot of details here. I do want to give you basic background knowledge, so you can explore it and study it more if it's interesting to you. Large multifamily, similar to a large mobile home park, is just completely different than single-family. Everything is different, from the way it's managed to the way it's financed.

There can be lots of reward but also lots of risk when it comes to large multifamily. Typically, your competition with apartments is other apartment communities. And these other apartment owners have deep pockets and it's a business for them, so you better believe they know their business. They look at reports and numbers beyond what an owner of a single-family home would typically look at.

One positive to owning a large multifamily property is that you can obtain non-recourse debt on it. That means that banks will finance these properties for long terms with fixed rates and not hold you personally liable for the debt. Basically, they are financing the property and the income it produces. However, they will want to know that the buyer is astute enough to run the project successfully. They want to know that you or one of your partners is experienced in owning and managing large properties. And in order to finance a large apartment complex, it would require you to put down millions of dollars as your down payment since you would be purchasing a multi-million-dollar property. So, if the project fails, you lose your down payment.

It's a numbers game when you get this big, so they are looking at occupancy rates, tracking the number of visitors to the community, and lots more. The large-scale apartment communities track metrics and look at things that you would never look at for a single-family. And if you try to enter that game and don't know what you are doing, the competition will put you out of business. The competition will know your numbers, and if they know them better than you, then they will dominate you. Again, it's completely different than owning a few or even a lot of single-family homes or condos.

If multifamily is something you are interested in, there are resources available for you to educate yourself. Most of us aren't going to have the resources to get into investing in large apartments. However, if you do, my recommendation would be to stay away from this type of investment until you consider yourself an experienced and sophisticated investor. Or, find a partner that is experienced, and you provide the funding while they provide the expertise.

STUDENT HOUSING

Student housing is not so much a type of property as it is a type of leasing. Since I'm located in a university community, we see a lot of student rentals. This source makes up a large percentage of the tenants in some communities. It could be anything from a two-bedroom unit to a five-bedroom and five-bathroom unit.

Student housing could be a large multifamily, but it could also be detached homes or condos. It's a variety. Some students are drawn to large crowds and amenities whereas others like the peace and quiet of a stand-alone structure. Keep that in mind when you are selecting your units as they attract different kinds of students with different behavioral standards.

One great thing about student housing is that if a student has the means to be in college, the parents are probably involved and are probably footing the bill. That means the parents can also pay the rent, and landlords typically will get a parental guarantee to back up the student on the lease. It's hard to approve an application for a full-time student with conventional qualifying guidelines because most students don't have jobs, or if they do, it's part-time and not making much money.

If you decide to invest in student rentals, I definitely recommend getting a parental guarantee. This makes your lease really strong and almost guarantees you'll collect your rent. In this case, you would be qualifying the parents and putting them on the hook to pay the rent. And if the parents are sending their kids to college, they typically have resources and can qualify for the lease.

Also, it's not likely that you'll keep the same tenants more than a couple of years. Occasionally, you'll see a group of students come in and rent the same place for four years, but it's rare. They typically come in with roommates, and as they go through their college career, they have fallouts with some and meet new friends. Students are constantly moving, so you might find yourself turning these units more often.

However, I had a great experience a few years ago with students until my gravy train finally ran out. I had a house leased to three grad students, and they were in different years of their education. As one would graduate and move on, the other roommates wanted to stay, so they would bring in a friend. Then when the next one graduated, the ones that were still in school would bring in another new friend. This went on for about six years, so even though the tenants were changing slightly and I was producing new leases, I didn't have to spend money on painting or cleaning for those years because they never officially moved out. It was great!

Student housing can be very lucrative, but it can also change rapidly. When you are in the student housing game, you really need to keep your finger on the pulse of what's going on with the campus, students, and new developments.

What I typically see in our area is that the community that is the most popular and most expensive this year will be replaced by a newer property with more amenities next year or in a few years. Then rent can sometimes fall in the property that's a few years old, as it is no longer attracting the highest-paying students. And as more units are built, the demand for the older ones declines. It really comes down to supply and demand. As new units are built, supply increases. If demand stays the same, rent rates may fall. If demand rises with supply, rents will remain steady. So, with student housing, you always want to know what's going on with enrollment and housing at the campus.

Rents can rise and fall, and demand can increase or decrease with student housing depending on the direction the university or college is going. If it's growing and they increase enrollment by 500 students in one year, that's 500 more bedrooms that are needed for that year. That can be great for owners of student rentals as the demand will increase and rents will likely rise. However, if the institution decides they are going to keep enrollment the same, but build a new 500-bedroom dormitory, then that decreases demand for private student housing and can make rents fall.

So, while student rentals can be very lucrative, it also has its risks. And what the campus or university does with their enrollment and housing is completely out of your control.

COMMERCIAL PROPERTY

While this book is primarily about residential properties, I would be amiss if I didn't touch on commercial. Commercial leasing definitely has its benefits and is preferred by some investors. Like large multifamily, it's just different and in my opinion should not be where you start.

Commercial real estate is anything from office space to warehouse space to retail space to restaurant space or even special purpose property. Drive through your city, and you'll see all kinds of different businesses in all kinds of different buildings. Those are all commercial properties. A few of them are probably owned by the businesses themselves, but the majority are leased by the businesses and owned by investors.

The benefit of owning commercial property is that because it's commercial, you are leasing to a business rather than an individual. If it's a reputable business or a large company, then collecting rent is almost guaranteed. While there is always the risk in residential that a tenant may lose a job and not be able to pay, it's not likely that a company would not be able to pay its rent unless the company goes bankrupt.

Anything is possible and renting to a small mom-and-pop-type operation probably isn't any safer than renting out a home or residence. However, if your tenant is a Fortune 500 company or a company that's traded on Wall Street, that rent is a drop in the bucket for them. So, commercial leasing offers some peace of mind for some investors.

I have leased my commercial property in the past to companies with multiple offices in multiple states, and I've also leased to local sole proprietors. They both paid rent and it worked out great. But, common sense tells you the odds are a smaller company would default before a large company.

Another great benefit for commercial leases is that the lease is almost always for more than one year. Commercial leases typically range from three to ten years. And sometimes they go to twenty years and beyond. If you lease a space to a large company, government entity, or something of the like for ten years, that's about as safe of an investment as you will find anywhere, and there is a benefit to that. A lease like that almost guarantees you receive a payment every month for 120 months! It's like an annuity.

The downside to leasing commercial space is that sometimes it can take months and months to fill, depending on the type of property. So, you must be prepared to handle several months of vacancies and not depend solely on the rent to make the bank payment or to pay your own bills.

Commercial property also may need major changes in order to make it fit for a particular business. One business may need larger or smaller rooms. A restaurant will need a kitchen, plumbing in different places, and lighting in different places. Because businesses are all so different, they are looking primarily for the right amount of space and the right location.

Sometimes the tenant will pay for these changes while other times they'll seek help from the landlord and they'll negotiate this with the lease. Depending on the market, often a commercial landlord will need to offer a tenant improvement allowance (TIA) in order to attract a tenant to a commercial space. This allowance will offset some of the cost the tenant will have to incur to ready the space. This is never done with residential.

So, if you decide to buy commercial property, remember—location, visibility, and the right amount of space is what they are looking for. Fill that demand, and it can prove to be a great investment.

LAND

Land is also a type of real estate that some investors like to buy. While I like land for a lot of reasons, I don't like it so much as only an investment. I do own some land, and I've bought it for speculative reasons. However, the downside to owing land is that normally, unless you do something creative, there is no cash flow. I like to invest for cash flow, and typically raw land doesn't give it to me.

I've had clients do very well buying and selling land. They buy and sell a few years later and make huge profits on land. So, while it can be lucrative, it's not what's going to set you free by paying you every month, so you can replace your salary. This is the strategy of many land buyers, to simply buy low and sell high. Some will subdivide it before selling because often the smaller parts are worth more than the whole, so that is a strategy.

You could use this strategy to increase your income over the short run to give you the capital needed to invest in your long-term cash flowing properties.

Other ways to make land pay is through growing crops or timber. If it's an annual crop that can be grown and sold each year, like fruit trees, then land can produce a return that way. However, raising crops requires much more management and labor than simply renting a space to a tenant. Some will grow timber, which is only harvested every 10 to 15 years and again at 25 to 30 years. Again, timber doesn't pay you every month or even every year, but only once every few years.

There are a few people out there who will purchase land below value and then owner finance it to individuals at an above-market price with above-average interest rates. This is one way that you could also make land work that creates cash flow. But again, you are divesting yourself of the asset because you are selling it, which means once they pay you off, the cash flow goes away.

The final way and best way to make land work as an investment is through a land lease. There's that word again . . . lease. That's what you want, and that's what will make you money every month. This is how you make land cash flow!

I own a piece of property with a land lease. It's leased to a billboard company. The nice thing about this lease is that I get a check every single month from the billboard company for a flat rate. They sell ads on the billboard, and they actually own the billboard. They pay to keep it maintained and lit. I simply own the dirt that it sits on, but because it's located on a major highway, the billboard company likes its visibility. They are able to lease the spot from me, sell ads on their board, and it's a win-win for us both. And I get paid whether or not they sell ads on it. I like it because I don't have to sell ads. I'm not in the ad-selling business. I get paid for owning the dirt underneath the billboard.

I like this investment because I never need to make a repair or do anything with it. I just get mailbox money every month. Another lease similar to a billboard would be for a cell phone tower.

Sometimes you see fast food restaurants and the like are built on land that is leased. Typically, these leases are for 99 years so that the restaurant knows they control the land long enough to justify putting a building on it. They do this because it frees up their cash and improves their balance sheet for operations. The companies like it because they don't have the debt associated with owning the land, but simply a lease.

Having a land lease in place can make land a great investment. Otherwise, you can still make money buying and selling land, but personally, I prefer to invest for cash flow. So, if I buy land, I do it with the intention of somehow producing steady income from it or by knowing that I'm speculating and limiting myself from buying another cash flowing property.

Most land is bought for speculation, and very few parcels are leased and produce a consistent cash-flowing income.

These are the major types of properties that we commonly see. Beyond the types, each type can be broken into different classes, so I want to touch briefly on the different classes of real estate. The classes are A, B, C, and D. These asset classes are most often used when referring to multifamily properties, but can be applied to any of the asset classes including single-family and commercial. Let's check them out.

ASSET CLASSES

You may have read or heard of more sophisticated investors or managers of large portfolios reference their business by stating they work in "B Class" apartments or "C Class" apartments or something like that. So, what does that really mean?

Within all types of real estate there are different classes. The classes are a grading system to indicate what type of property it is. You could compare it to getting your essays graded when you were in school or grading of consumer goods or anything else. Of course, the grade can vary depending on who is giving the grade. Just as with a research paper in school, one teacher could give it a B whereas another might give it a C+. So the classes can be subjective to a degree.

Typically A Class real estate refers to high-end and more luxury-type units. B Class is a step below that, and C Class is below that. As you get into D Class, typically the buildings are old, in need of repair, and you are in areas that might have high crime and other problems to make them less desirable.

You will find that often these classes are loosely defined by investors and real estate agents. You may find some properties that are marginal and may be borderline with some people calling them a C and others a B.

Here are the definitions of each class as referenced by Biggerpockets .com.[9] This site actually grades locations as well as properties.

Class A Location—the newest and hottest part of town with the highest priced real estate, wealthiest people, and best schools.

Class A Real Estate—these are typically newer properties that are less than 10 years old with few maintenance issues. They have modern finishes, such as granite countertops, wood floors, and other in-demand amenities. They typically command more rent but less cash flow because of a higher purchase cost. These are seen as "easy investments."

Class B Location—not as nice and desirable as Class A but still near good schools and restaurants. These are middle-class areas and will attract blue-collar workers.

Class B Real Estate—typically 10 to 30 years old and mostly upgraded but lacking the shine of a Class A property. Rental income is lower than Class A, and maintenance costs are higher due to the age of the property.

Class C Location—likely a lower-income area with homes that are 30 years old or more. This area attracts people with low-wage jobs and some government subsidies. You'll also see a lot of check-cashing and pawnshops in these areas.

Class C Real Estate—properties that are older than 30 years and look like it. They typically need repairs, and maintenance is ongoing. Systems in the home may be outdated and require attention. Rents are typically low and more affordable than A or B Class.

Class D Location—these locations are areas of high crime and drug use. There could be several buildings with boarded-up windows and vacant properties. These are not the kinds of areas you want to travel alone in.

Class D Real Estate—these properties are very old, like Class C, but have far more neglect and are barely habitable, needing significant repairs. The rent is exceptionally cheap, but getting good tenants is near impossible as the area can be dangerous.

Biggerpockets.com also included a comment in a forum that I really like written by Matt R. This is Matt R.'s quick and easy way for us to think of and distinguish the properties.

Class A—you and your family would live in it.

Class B—you and your family could live in it.

Class C—you and your family could live in it if it was an emergency.

Class D—you would rather be camping.

That about sums it up!

So, once you determine whether you want to focus on single-family homes, condos, mobile homes, multifamily, commercial, or whatever, you also need to decide if you want to focus on a certain class of that asset. There is no right or wrong answer as to what type of investment is right for you.

As you meet other investors, you'll learn that some love A Class and swear by it whereas others only want to look at C Class. And believe it or not, there are some landlords who love D Class properties. These might be what some would call slumlords.

Generally speaking, A Class properties will need very little repair and attract the highest-paying and higher-income tenants. However, these properties also cost more to purchase and generally have a lower return on investment. The tradeoff is that you have security in knowing that you won't likely be surprised by costly repairs, and the tenants have high incomes and are likely to always pay on time. However, sometimes these higher income tenants can have higher expectations and make demands for property improvements that other tenants might not make.

As you get into the lower classes of property, the return on investment will likely be higher when you look at the ratio between purchase price and rents received. However, you will likely see more repairs and also may have more defaults on leases, more late payments, etc. The A Class spectrum is very little risk with smaller returns, and as you move down the spectrum to D Class, there is more risk and more management intensity with the possibility of higher returns.

There are pros and cons to each of the classes of real estate. Personally, I've settled into preferring more of a B Class and occasionally some high C Class properties for my portfolio. You'll need to determine what's ideal for your individual situation. Your personality, risk tolerance, and overall financial goals will push you in one direction or another.

Sometimes finding a Class B or C property in an improving location can be ideal for appreciation and can sometimes prove to be a good investment. Look for properties in locations that you think are not A Class areas now, but that you think will be in the future. Whatever you do, don't overthink it because you can't predict the future. Investigate properties and settle into what's the right fit for you. Look for your desired ROI, consider your risk tolerance, and then invest for the cash flow.

As you begin to analyze properties, you'll rank them by class. So, what's important to analyze? In the next chapter, we'll consider the important factors for you to analyze as you begin shopping for investment real estate.

CHAPTER 5
Analyzing Investment Properties

As you begin looking at investment real estate that fits your preferred niche and asset class, you'll realize that no two pieces of real estate are exactly alike. You'll notice that some are better in some ways whereas others trump in other areas. You need to decide what's most important to you and rank these properties to determine what's best for you. And you need to know how to analyze the numbers, calculate your returns, and determine what's going to be the best investment for you. What's best for you might not be best for me, and vice versa.

Let me start by saying, I'm going to try keep it simple in this chapter. When you really get deep into analyzing numbers in commercial real estate and large multi-million-dollar transactions, you'll find there are all sorts of formulas and ratios to consider. You can easily get lost in the calculations. One such calculation is the internal rate of return, which is very precise and a great formula to use on large projects. It incorporates the projected appreciation of a property, the debt reduction each year, the depreciation, and future cash flows into the equation. It's very complex and detailed, but you'll see it used on commercial appraisals and sometimes on a large-scale pro forma. I only mention it because many sophisticated investors believe it's truly the most accurate and best formula for analyzing property. I wouldn't disagree, but it's just too much for the average investor to consider. And personally, I don't use it.

While some sophisticated investors would say that you need more calculations to really understand the return of an investment, I like to keep it simple. They have a valid point when you are analyzing deals that are in the tens of millions. For our purposes of investing on a much smaller scale, it's simply not necessary. I want to show you a couple of simple formulas that you can use to objectively compare one real estate investment with another and to compare a real estate investment with another alternative, such as a stock or bond.

The two metrics that I want to explain in this chapter are cash-on-cash return (CoC) and capitalization rate, or cap rate. I'll give the formulas for each and show you how to use each. The end goal is to maximize your return on investment (ROI). This is typically done in two ways. One: you rent out the property, and the ROI is the amount of cash the property generates each year on an annual basis. Two: when the property is sold, you get an ROI. The ROI when sold can only be calculated backwards because until you sell, you don't really know the sales price. You can estimate it if you prefer, and that's what some of the more complex formulas include. However, I like to focus on the annual return from rents, which is more predictable and certain.

To simplify your calculations of cap rate, cash-on-cash return and to compare several properties, download a free Rental Property ROI Calculator Tool by going to www.TheRealEstateWayBook.com/gift.

CASH-ON-CASH RETURN

When I'm trying to decide whether to buy a property, I focus primarily on the return on investment (ROI) by calculating the cash-on-cash return based on rents received. This is the percentage of cash that returns per year in relation to the amount of cash invested in the property. To determine this, you need to figure out the net amount of money the property could generate after expenses and debt service each year. I call this cash flow. The formula to determine cash flow is:

Total Income – Operating Expenses – Debt Service = CASH FLOW

Cash flow is what's left over after you receive rent and pay all expenses, including debt service. Income is the amount of rent the property receives. Operating expenses include things like taxes, insurance, and repairs. Debt service is the mortgage you may have on the property.

While some may consider net operating income (NOI) the same as cash flow, most of the formulas you find for calculating NOI don't include the debt service. Reality is that if you are financing a property, you must pay the debt service, so I include that in any cash-on-cash calculations. Of course, if you don't finance, then your debt service would simply be zero.

First and foremost, your cash flow must be a positive number. Otherwise, you are setting yourself up for failure and will most likely lose money every year. When determining whether to buy a property, what matters isn't just the positive cash flow it could produce, but the return on investment (ROI) it delivers. This is the figure that will show you if one investment is better than another and help you to determine whether paying cash or leveraging with financing is a better option for acquiring the property.

To simplify it, think of it this way: when I take a hard-earned dollar and invest it in a piece of real estate, how much of it comes back to me each year? If it's 25%, then that means I'd get $0.25 back for every dollar invested each year, which is a great return. Essentially, with this scenario, in four years, I would have my initial investment back. This is calculated by using the formula for cash-on-cash return:

CASH-ON-CASH RETURN = Cash Flow / Total Cash Invested

To determine a property's cash-on-cash return there are two variables you must know: cash flow and total cash invested. I already gave the formula for determining the cash flow. The total cash investment depends on how you initially buy the property: paying for it completely in cash upfront or doing some kind of financing. With a cash purchase the whole price is the total cash investment. If you are doing some kind of financing to buy the real estate, the total investment made would equal the amount of money you put down to get the financing; for most lenders, this amount is around 20% of the purchase price. The resulting cash-on-cash return will be different depending on how you go about purchasing the property.

For clarity, let's look at some scenarios, so you can see how to calculate the cash-on-cash return and also to see why it's such a useful number in helping you figure out whether to buy a property.

Scenario A

Let's say you purchase a rental house for $100K, and it rents for $1,000 per month or $12,000 per year. After paying taxes, insurance, repairs, and management fees, you calculate the operating expenses to be $4,000 total. Thus, you are left with $8,000 per year. Let's say you buy the house for cash. This means your total investment made is $100K, and you get back $8,000 in cash flow per year.

CASH FLOW = $12,000 (income) – $4,000 (expenses)
– 0 (no debt service) = $8,000

CoC RETURN = $8,000 / $100,000 = 8%

This means for every one dollar you invested into the property, you get $0.08 back each year. It's an 8% simple return each year (this does not include tax benefits from depreciation and the appreciation in the house's value).

Scenario B

Using the same house as above, let's say you use financing and put down $20K. In this case, you would have the same expenses as above, but let's assume your mortgage payment (debt service) is $450 per month or $5,400 per year. You actually only return $2,600 in cash flow per year (see calculations below). However, your initial total cash investment was only $20K. So, you returned $2,600 cash on a cash investment of $20K. Let's look at the cash-on-cash return for this scenario.

CASH FLOW = $12,000 (income) – $4,000 (expenses) – $5,400 (debt service) = $2,600

CoC RETURN = $2,600 / $20,000 = 13%

This means for every one dollar you've put into the property, you get $0.13 back. Again, this is a simple annual return without factoring in tax depreciation or appreciation of the property.

So, as you can see, scenario B actually gives you a higher return on the cash you invested than scenario A. Now, scenario B also comes with the burden of carrying debt and having a payment to make. So, each investor has to decide for themselves on whether or not to leverage with financing as shown in scenario B to get the higher cash-on-cash return.

Where the CoC formula falls short is that it fails to take into account a few other factors. These factors are depreciation on taxes (discussed in chapter 10), interest deduction on taxes (chapter 10), and principal pay-down (as you make payments each year the loan balance is reduced). All of these factors make the investment described in scenario B more attractive. So technically, the return on this investment would be higher than 13%. If you are more analytical and want to go deeper, the more complex formulas will work out these returns in more detail.

The second opportunity for a cash-on-cash return on this investment is when you sell. Let's say you sell it after 10 years. It's now worth $150K.

SCENARIO A—WHEN YOU SELL

For those ten years, you've been making an 8% cash-on-cash return from renting as calculated already in scenario A. However, because you sell it for $50K more than what you bought it for ($150K – $100K), this makes for an additional return. Let's calculate it.

**CASH-ON-CASH RETURN FROM SELLING =
(Sales Price – Purchase Price) / Total Cash Investment,
which is equivalent to $50,000 / $100,000 = 50%**

- Because it's over a 10-year period, the annual CoC return from selling is an additional 5% (50% / 10 years).

- To get the total annual cash-on-cash return, we add up the CoC return from renting and from selling, 8% + 5%, which ends up being a 13% total ROI each year.

Realistically though, there is no way to know for sure how much you will sell it for in 10 years until that day actually comes. So, looking back we can see the total return on investment whereas when we are making the initial investment, we must only look at the annual returns from cash flow. This is why I recommend investing for annual cash flow and letting the appreciation be a bonus. But, this is a very realistic scenario, so as you can see, appreciation can be a huge bonus!

SCENARIO B—WHEN YOU SELL

In scenario B when you sell, you still make an additional $50K, but this time it was on an initial investment of $20K.

$$\textbf{CASH-ON-CASH RETURN FOR SELLING} = \$50{,}000 \;/\; \$20{,}000$$
$$= 250\%$$

- Because it's over a 10-year period, the yearly ROI based on the CoC return from selling is 25% (250% / 10).

- To get the total yearly cash-on-cash return, we add up the yearly CoC return from renting and from selling, 13% + 25%, for a total of a 38% return on investment! Are your current investments making a return like this?

Is this return even possible? Yes! These kinds of returns happen all the time in real estate. And because you can leverage with real estate, you can amplify your returns greatly as in the scenario above. I recommend you use debt wisely, but it can definitely be an accelerator to your returns when applied appropriately.

Now, this higher return will not be realized until you sell, but the same goes for a stock or any other asset that appreciates in value. It must be sold to convert the appreciation into cash.

You may be wondering if this kind of appreciation is typical. Home prices have risen significantly over the past several years. While prices dipped during the Great Recession, over the long term, they definitely have increased significantly. See the chart below from the US Census.[10]

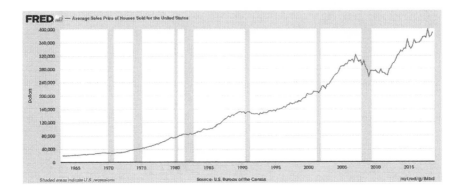

By principle, I never depend on appreciation to make a deal work. Appreciation is an unknown and uncontrollable factor. Based on history, it's almost guaranteed, but I always consider appreciation as a bonus. And as you can see, it can be a big bonus! If the numbers work on the front side of the equation, by analyzing CoC return from rental cash flow, then I'm happy. That's the calculation I like to use to determine whether or not I will invest in a property.

CAP RATE

Capitalization rate, or cap rate, is another way to analyze properties. This is primarily used in commercial real estate, but also it can be applied to investment property. Don't get too hung up on this, but if you are buying investment properties, it's a term you will hear and you need to know what it is.

Cap rate is simply a standardized way to evaluate properties and is calculated the same way independent of any debt service. Debt service doesn't affect cap rate. However, cap rate is a way to quickly and easily compare one property to another.

The formula for calculating the cap rate is as follows:

NET OPERATING INCOME (NOI) =
Total Income – Operating Expenses (not including debt service)

*CAP RATE = Net Operating Income (NOI)/Total Price of Property

*Note: This cap rate is equivalent to the CoC return when paying the full price in cash.

In the previously given scenarios A and B, for both, the cap rate is 8%. Whether there is debt on it or not, the cap rate is 8%, calculated as:

NOI = $12,000 (income) – $4,000 (expenses) = $8,000

CAP RATE = $8,000 (NOI) / $100,000 (total price) = 8%

If you were comparing this investment to another that, say, cost $150K to purchase and generated $1,500 per month in income, or $18,000 per year, with $7,000 in expenses for an NOI of $11,000 per year, then you might initially think it's a better investment because it generates more cash each year. However, a quick cap rate calculation would prove otherwise.

CAP RATE = $11,000 (NOI) / $150,000 (total price) = 7.3%

The cap rate helps you to quickly compare two investments. I recommend you analyze them further, but it can be used to narrow down options when you are shopping for real estate. And cap rate is a universal term in investment real estate, so you need to understand it.

This formula is often used in reverse to value properties. If you are preparing to sell a property or even comparing certain classes of properties in an area, you'll find cap rate useful. The cap rate can be used to determine the price of a property, as given in this formula:

PROPERTY VALUE = NOI / Cap Rate

For example, let's say you've owned an office building for a while and you are trying to determine the value of it to determine if you might want to sell. You talk to several commercial agents and appraisers to learn that office buildings are currently trading around a 7% cap rate. You can then determine the value of a particular property based on the income it's generated.

Let's say an office building generates $8,000 per month or $96K per year, and this is the net income after expenses. If properties like this are trading at a 7% cap rate, what would be a fair price for it?

$96,000 (NOI) / .07 (cap rate) = $1,371,429 (property value)

Any price above $1,371,429 would be less than a 7% cap rate, and any price lower would be higher than a 7% cap rate. When you initially begin to compare properties, you can use cap rate to do the comparisons. Then you begin to consider other factors such as location, length of leases, condition of the property, etc., to determine if the value should be higher or lower. The cap rate just gives you a standard way to quickly evaluate properties.

If office buildings are trading at a 6% cap rate, then the value increases. It would look like this:

$96,000 (cash flow) / .06 (cap rate) = $1,600,000 (property value)

Can you see how this formula can be used to standardize and compare properties? Again, it's primarily used in commercial real estate, like retail, office, and industrial, but you'll also see it in residential properties from time to time.

LOOK CLOSELY AT THE NUMBERS

Make sure that you look closely at the full financials anytime a cap rate is given. Many real estate agents will use the gross income (before expenses) rather than the net income (after expenses) to make this calculation. For example, the house that rents for $12,000 with $4,000 in expenses, only nets $8,000 per year. If the price is $100K, then it's an 8% cap rate. However, some agents will use the $12,000 gross income figure and call it a 12% cap rate. They do this to try and make the investment look more attractive. Some investors who are inexperienced or don't know how to calculate the numbers for themselves may get taken for a ride. So, don't fall for it!

If you buy a property thinking it's a 12% cap but really it's an 8% cap, then you'll end up disappointed. So, don't take their word for it. Verify expenses and do your due diligence.

Present or Future?

As mentioned already, my personal focus is on the monthly cash flow and cash-on-cash return on an investment. Some investors prefer to put more weight on what they believe will be the future appreciation, and some do very well with this approach. When you begin shopping and choosing properties, you'll need to decide if you want to focus your ROI on maximizing annual returns from cash flow (i.e., rental income after expenses) or if you want to bet on hitting it big with appreciation. In most cases, you'll enjoy the benefits of both cash flow and appreciation. However, you might decide to pay a little more for a property with a lower annual return from cash flow, if you feel confident the property will appreciate greatly in the coming years due to the growth of an area or some other factor. Remember, anytime you invest for appreciation only, you are gambling to a degree.

Because the future amount of appreciation is unpredictable, I like to maximize my ROI on an annual basis through cash flow and cash-on-cash return. My focus is annual (or monthly) cash flow, which means the property must be purchased at a price such that the rents give me the return that I'm looking for. As noted already, I view appreciation as a bonus. For other investors I know, they invest primarily for anticipated appreciation. They simply want the property to be cash flow positive each month, even if it only makes them $1.00 per month. They plan, or hope, to cash in and make a great return when they sell. Their focus is on anticipated appreciation rather than annual returns. Again, in my opinion, this type of investing is riskier because it is speculating on an unknown future. However, some do very well with this approach. They feel they can "see" the future, and many of these people do have vision. They go with their gut and are successful. It's just not as predictable as investing for the annual returns.

As you can imagine, a property that is right for one investor to purchase as an investment might not be right for me or you. On the same hand, something that might be a good fit for me may not look like a winner for you or for other investors. Each of us is drawn to different aspects. The greater point I'm trying to make clear is that there are lots of ways to make money in real estate and each person will place more importance on certain aspects.

ALWAYS ON THE UP AND UP

One of the best things about owning rental property is that your annual returns are almost guaranteed to rise over time. Whereas the annual returns from the stock market might go up or down, your returns on real estate should only go up with time. Rents go up in time. Have you ever seen them go down? To see this point demonstrated, look to the following chart showing how the rents in the US have risen over the 11 year period from 2005-2016.[11]

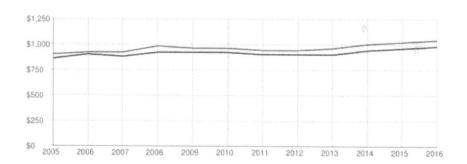

Average Rent 2005 = $901
Average Rent 2016 = $1,050
Top Line = Average Rent
Bottom Line = Median Rent

Fortunately, the rents on my properties have gone from averaging about $950 to $1,300 per month over the past 10 years, which is an increase of about $350 per property per month, which equates to $4,200 per year per property! Rents will rise at different rates in different locations. But, you can expect rents to rise, which means a higher cash flow and higher net income as time goes by. So, with time, the return on your initial investment only gets higher. This is why I say real estate is a more stable and more predictable investment than investing in the stock market.

THE BIG 5

There are five major components of real estate that contribute to its value and to the ROI that I like to evaluate and analyze when I'm considering a purchase. And I like to re-analyze these things from time to time to make sure I want to keep a property or sell it and replace it with something better.

The five factors that contribute to ROI are:

1. Location

2. Property Condition and Price

3. Desirability

4. Functionality

5. Market Rent

Each of these factors must be taken into account when evaluating a property, and each investor will value each of these factors differently.

You'll need to decide which of the factors will have priority when you are shopping for a home to buy. Is location more important to you or property condition? Or are you strictly looking at the current price-to-rent ratio with little regard to the other factors? In my opinion, you need to consider them all, but for each individual investor, the factors will have more or less importance, and carry more or less weight.

FACTOR 1—LOCATION

Let's start by discussing location. There is an old adage in real estate that I'm sure you've heard: "Location, location, location." While location is not the only factor to analyze, it is a big one. And it's one that you can never change. The location is always static. What happens around the property might increase or decrease its value over time.

Earlier, I stated that I invest for cash flow, trying to maximize the ROI, and not for appreciation. However, location often has the biggest influence on whether or not a property will appreciate. Plus, properties in great locations will be desirable to rent as well. So, if you can buy property in a great location, with a high probability of its value going up, why wouldn't you do it?

A property that is in a desirable location and one that becomes more desirable will benefit you in both price appreciation and rent appreciation. This is always a good thing. So be sure to select properties that are in good locations. Often, we find that location will trump other factors. However, you also have to view location with respect to other variables.

Properties located in areas that are growing with lots of new construction going on in the area, lots of jobs being created, companies moving in, etc., will typically go up in value. Properties that are conveniently located near shopping, restaurants, and entertainment are generally more desirable and have higher odds of appreciation. The school zone where a property is located also will have a bearing on its value, rentability, and the market rent.

The difficult part of buying in a great location is that often the price is higher for that area. Sometimes it can make sense to sacrifice the best location if the other factors are where you want them and the property meets your other standards. Often price is too high in the best locations when compared with the market rent. If the price is too high, rent is too low, and cash flow is too low, the ROI will be less, so it might not make the cut.

So, it's finding the right balance. A property in a high crime area, for example, will be harder to lease and will rent for less money. While it can also likely be purchased for less, it has little potential to appreciate unless the area changes in time.

So, while location is a big factor, it must be considered along with the other factors as well.

FACTOR 2—PROPERTY CONDITION

The property condition relative to price is also a huge factor to consider. If you don't get this part right, you could end up overpaying for the property. On the flip side, you could also find a great deal. And you need to know whether it's a deal or not. You should look at enough properties online, doing drive-bys, and even walking through some places that you know what you can get for the price in your market. That way, when you find a deal, you immediately know it.

If you are working with an expert real estate agent, like the ones on my team, you'll get the needed guidance to help you determine which homes offer the most value.

Price and condition are directly correlated. The better the condition of a home, the higher price it will capture. As the house needs work, price will go down. Often the homes that need the most work can provide you with the most upside when you are looking at overall value. But, if you buy a home that needs repair, you have to be willing to make the investment to bring it up to par. When buying in this way, you are also taking risks of repair overruns and spending more than you intend.

If you can find a house that you can buy for 60% to 70% of its after-repair value (ARV) and you spend 10% to 20% to repair it, then you are in a great position of equity once you complete the repairs. That will give you lots of options with regard to financing and for leverage with lenders to buy more properties. We'll get into the financing portion in a future chapter, but if you are comfortable making repairs, consider homes that need work.

Most of the properties that I've personally purchased have been undervalued and in need of repair. In fact, the first rental house I purchased, I bought for $45K. It needed work. I spent about $15,000 to repair it, and it appraised for $75K after I was done, so I was able to refinance it, borrowing $60K, and getting all of my initial investment back.

BREAKDOWN: $45,000 (price) + $15,000 (repairs) = $60,000 total investment

The bank would finance 80%.

APPRAISED VALUE = $75,000 * 80% = $60,000 loan

I still have that house today, and I receive a rent check from it every month. I have an infinite return on that property since I was able to pull my initial cash investment back out. The mortgage balance is considerably lower now than it was when I purchased it.

I haven't used this strategy on all of my properties, but it's one that works and allows you to leverage and continue buying homes. We'll get into more details on this strategy in the next chapter.

If you have more money than time, a better strategy might just be to purchase a home that's move-in ready and then rent it out. You don't have instant equity in this case, but you can still achieve a great return on your money and you don't have to worry about scheduling contractors and taking the risk of unknown repairs. This is a safer and less risky strategy.

For example, my real estate brokerage recently represented a builder who was building starter homes in a subdivision. Most of the buyers were young families or young single people just starting out in life. A few of them were empty nesters who were downsizing. However, two of the buyers were investors. They saw these homes as a great opportunity to purchase a brand-new home that should not need repairs for 10 years or so, and would need very little maintenance during that time. They saw it as a consistent stream of revenue each month without surprise repairs because everything was new. And because everything was new, that's also very attractive to tenants. It was a great fit for their investment strategy. And they should see a return of around 9% per year, which is much better than you'll get from a bank. Plus, this doesn't factor in the likely appreciation. In fact, one house resold in the subdivision a year later for about 10% more than it was purchased for and I expect these homes will be worth much more in years to come as the price of construction materials continues to rise.

Everyone will be drawn to and have different preferences when it comes to investing. That's why there is no right or wrong answers as to what is or is not a good investment. Some people see things differently and value different things, so what works for one person won't work for another and vice versa.

When it comes to the condition of the home you are leasing out, just remember that the kind of tenants you want to attract want a nice, safe, and clean place to live. So, make sure the unit is clean with fresh paint and modern conveniences. Everything doesn't have to be new, but make sure it's clean and in relatively good condition. If the property you purchase doesn't meet these standards, make sure you budget for improving it.

If you try to lease properties in poor condition, you will only attract the tenants who will settle for anything and you will get less rent. These are typically the tenants that won't qualify for nicer homes, and they take what they can get. They generally will not care for your property as well as a tenant with higher expectations. Make the extra effort to provide a nice place, and you'll attract great tenants.

FACTOR 3—DESIRABILITY

Desirability is another factor that must be considered. Desirability can have a lot of different definitions. What's desirable to you may not be desirable to a future tenant. So, look for what's important to tenants and not necessarily to you.

I've always advised clients against buying very unique or odd properties. They may be drawn to the charm and character or certain aspects of the property, and that's great. A renter could be drawn to it as well. However, typically, unique properties can take longer to lease when they don't appeal to the masses. Generally speaking, you want to appeal to the largest pool of potential prospects possible. This will drive up demand and the rent rate.

FACTOR 4—FUNCTIONALITY

Also consider the functionality of the residential units that you invest in. If there is a functional deficiency, it will affect the desirability of the house, the rent rate, and the time it takes to find qualified tenants.

For example, if a three-bedroom home only has one bathroom, it will rent for less than one that has two bathrooms. It's a functionality thing. Modern day tenants prefer more bathrooms. If a master bathroom is really small or the closet is really small, it will rent, but a home with larger bathrooms and closets will rent for more and will likely stay rented for longer. It's all about supplying what your customer, the tenant, is looking for.

Another deficiency that we sometimes see is a two-story house that has the master bedroom on the main level and only one bathroom on the main level. There will be an entry from the master bedroom and also to the main area. I grew up in a house like this, but today, most people don't want to use their master bathroom as their guest bathroom. So, houses that have a half bath on the main level are more desirable, will rent for more, and will sell for more.

If the home doesn't have access to high speed Internet, for example, that could be a functional issue for some tenants, especially if they are younger or if they work from home. If you are in a big city, lack of Internet may be hard for you to imagine, but it's common in some rural areas, so take this into consideration.

Things like small closets and bathrooms can be hard to remedy in a cost-effective way. It costs a lot to enlarge the footprint of a house, so unless you can expand into another room, it could be a functional deficiency.

Again, it's all relative to the price you pay, as a home with smaller baths and more functional problems will typically sell for less as well, which means you can buy it for less. So, I'm not saying don't buy a house with small bathrooms or closets. I'm simply saying to factor this in with the price you pay, the amount of rent it will bring, and look at the overall picture.

Even homes with functional deficiencies will rent. They will just rent for less, may take longer to lease, and not have as much demand for them. However, if you are able to buy one at a great price, it may be OK. All of these factors have to be taken together and considered.

Are you starting to see how my descriptions may fit into the definitions of the different classes: A, B, C, and D? The A properties will be desirable in every way with no deficiencies, while the C Class may have some less desirable features but will cost much less. Use your own grading system based on what you put priority on to select and grade your potential properties.

Factor 5—Market Rent

Finally, consider the amount of rent you can get and how it stacks up with the other factors. The amount of rent will be correlated with the location, condition, supply and demand, and class of property. You want to be able to get maximum rent for your investment, and you want to be able to lease it quickly to a qualified tenant. And not only lease it quickly this year, but in years to come. You want to be able to collect that rent and also not pour money into it like a money pit. You need to analyze all aspects.

My recommendation also is not to be the cheapest rent in your town, but you also don't want to be the most expensive. If you have the cheapest rent, you will attract the bottom feeders. However, if you are on the higher end, you typically see the law of diminishing returns at work. What I mean by that is once you get on the high end of the rent range, many people who can afford that rate will just buy a home instead of rent one. So, your pool of prospects is smaller and your competition is not only other rental homes, but also homes for sale.

Think through each of these factors and decide what you are going to give more weight to when you are analyzing properties for your next purchase. What's most important to you?

Now that you know the niche of real estate you want to invest in, the asset class you want to invest in, and your investment criteria, we can look into how to find the best deals, the subject of the next chapter.

CHAPTER 6
Finding Deals

Where do you find the right properties for sale? First, you need to be clear on what it is you are looking for. If you don't know what you are looking for, it's going to be very difficult to find. If you have a clear picture of the ideal property, then it's going to jump out at you when you come across it.

Now that we've gone over the different types and classes of real estate, you'll need to zero in on what fits your goals. What type of real estate is going to be best for you? It will vary between investors, and each will have their own opinion on what's best. Some, like myself, really like single-family homes due to their stability. Even among single-family investors, some like A Class because it's easier whereas others like C Class for higher returns. Personally, I like B Class, but I will consider A or C if the numbers are favorable.

Other investors hate single-family and opt to pursue multifamily or commercial real estate. Some love land, and others love mobile home parks. You've got to determine your niche and then go find the best deals within that category.

FOUR CRUCIAL QUESTIONS

Before you can start looking for deals, answer the following questions to determine your niche:

1. What kind of real estate do I want to focus on? It can be any of the niches already described or a combination thereof:

- Single-family, condo/townhome, mobile home, mobile home park, duplex, triplex, quadraplex, apartment building, commercial retail, commercial office, land, etc.

2. What class of properties suits me best?

- Class A because of less risk and more stability

- Class C or D because I want the possibility of a higher return on investment, I'm up to the challenge of managing a more difficult situation, and I'm comfortable with the risk

- Or somewhere in-between, like Class B

3. How do I prioritize the five criteria?

- Location, condition, desirability, functionality, and market rental rate

4. What kind of return on my investment do I want?

- 5%, 7%, 8%, 10%, 15% or somewhere in between

Obviously, you want the highest ROI possible, but you must be realistic in your requirements. And, are you calculating your ROI with only the net income from rent, or are you factoring in an estimated appreciation? You must define what you are looking for here. Different returns can be expected in different locations throughout the country and among the real estate classes as we've learned.

Also, whether you leverage with debt or pay cash will change your ROI. Using debt can increase the return on your investment significantly in some cases, but it also comes with a little more risk and a little more hassle.

Once you have firmly answered these questions and clearly defined your real estate niche, you are ready to go shopping for an investment property. You can find many properties online while others you may find by driving around and seeing a sign or by word of mouth.

BELOW-MARKET GEMS & MOTIVATED SELLERS

When I buy personally and when I'm working for a client, I like to find deals that are below market or have some kind of upside where equity can be created very rapidly. In a good economy, it's more difficult to find these kinds of deals. In a bad economy, it is much easier. This is due to a combination of the fact that there are simply fewer deals when the economy is good, but also the fact that more buyers are competing for the properties when the economy is good. The opposite is true in a bad economy.

Sources of these kinds of promising deals may be foreclosed homes, homeowners who are behind on their payments, homeowners who are facing a need to move quickly due to job or health reasons, inherited property or property in an estate, sellers going through a divorce, or even other investors who have a bad property manager or are having a hard time managing it themselves.

Life happens. And life events can create motivated sellers who would love to sell their homes fast. Often health reasons and divorces motivate sellers to sell quickly and for a good price. Heirs who inherit properties often want to liquidate them as soon as possible so that they can get the cash to pay for other things. Many times, they don't want the property and are willing to sell at a discount.

As an investor, you want to buy from people who no longer want the property. Those are the motivated sellers. In a lot of cases, if there are multiple heirs, a few of them are motivated to sell quickly and others want to hold out for top dollar. So, it can create an interesting dynamic. Bottom line, when you are buying a home, you have to find a solution that is a win-win for you and the seller.

I've also bought property from other investors. We'll talk about property management in chapters 11 and 12, but good management can make the real estate game work whereas bad management can cause you to lose your mind and your money. In one particular instance, I bought a property from an investor whose property had lots of potential, but it was under-rented and not in great condition simply because the property manager was not doing a good job. The property manager was not trying to maximize this owner's profit. This house was under-rented by about $500 per month, so it really wasn't making money for the investor. And, because the manager hadn't taken care of basic repairs, it wasn't attracting the best tenants, which meant it wasn't being taken care of as it should be, somewhat of a downward spiral. This investor was frustrated and just wanted out. It created an opportunity for me.

Foreclosed properties can be a great way to get deals. Obviously, banks don't want properties, and they want them sold. The process is different in every state, but in Georgia, ads for such properties are run in the local newspaper and the properties are sold at auction. This is about the riskiest way possible to buy houses, and I don't recommend it for new investors.

There are two problems with buying homes this way. The first is that you are buying "as is." Often these homes still have people living in them. Even if they are vacant, you aren't given access to them prior to purchase and you have no way of getting them inspected, so it's high risk. Some of them are completely trashed and some have major problems. I've seen homes like this have major structural problems that can't be identified without entering the property. It's "as is, where is," and unexpected repairs can add up quickly. They must be purchased at a price low enough to justify lots of possible repairs.

The second problem with buying this way is that you must have cash on hand immediately. Buying this way is not an option for most people. Sophisticated investors sometimes do well buying this way, but I've also seen people overpay and lose tens of thousands of dollars. Furthermore, if there are liens on the property, they are inherited by the buyer. Liens are when money is owed on a property. A mortgage is a type of lien. However, liens can also be placed on real estate for non-payment of taxes or other bills. If work is done to a house that's not paid for, the contractor can place a workman's lien against the house. Generally, when the mortgage holder is foreclosing due to non-payment, it's the liens that are superior, and recorded prior to, the one foreclosing that will stay with the property. You don't want to purchase a property thinking you got a great deal, only to find out later that you now owe a past debt to another mortgage lender or to the government for unpaid taxes.

When buying real estate traditionally through a real estate closing attorney or title company, they investigate and make sure the title is clear. When buying at a bank auction, there is not a traditional closing. You are essentially buying the bank's position at the auction, so you inherit anything outstanding. In this way, you may think you bought a great deal only to find out there is a lien that stays with the property, and that now you own it, it's up to you to pay it off. It could be thousands of dollars. Due to the nature of buying this way, it's a lot easier to make a mistake and lose money. Again, this method is not ideal for the novice investor.

Most of the time, no one buys these properties at auction, and they go back to the bank as bank-owned inventory. Then, the bank will list them for sale with a real estate agent or on their website. Most will list with a real estate agent, and it will be on a multiple listing service and home search websites, so you can watch for these foreclosures to come on the open market or have your agent be watching for you. Once they are listed in this fashion, buyers are able to buy more traditionally, have inspections, make sure a title is clear, etc. I've personally bought and helped clients buy several bank-owned homes over the years. This is still a risky way to buy properties, but it's much safer and less risky than buying at auction.

If you are able to find owners who are behind on their payments, you can sometimes buy directly from them prior to foreclosure. At my real estate firm, we often get calls like this from motivated sellers. If we are representing them, of course, we try to get them the best price possible. However, more important than the best price, is getting them a buyer that will for sure close prior to foreclosure. Once the house forecloses, the owners would get nothing. Selling and getting them some money is better than them losing it all.

Recently my team at Woodall Realty Group had clients who were about to lose their home to foreclosure. They didn't tell us that in the beginning, so we were trying to get them top dollar. We actually got it under contract with a buyer who planned to move into it.

However, because they were a retail buyer, they asked for a long list of repairs after the home inspection. The seller then confided in us that they could not do repairs because they didn't have the money and that they would actually lose the house to foreclosure if it didn't sell within the next 3 to 4 weeks. When the seller refused repairs, the buyer terminated the contract. That meant we had to sell it again and close within 3 weeks to prevent foreclosure.

We ended up selling to an investor at a discount just prior to foreclosure. The sellers were happy because they avoided foreclosure and walked away with about $20K at closing. If a few more weeks had passed, they would have gotten nothing. The investor was happy because he got a great house with equity.

Could the seller have sold it for more? Sure. If they had funds and time to get repairs done or if they could continue making the mortgage payment. But they didn't, and they were quickly running out of time. For them, they were happy to get $20K profit instead of losing it all in foreclosure. This was a situation where my team truly created a win-win for everyone involved. That's how we like to do things in my brokerage.

It may sound cruel to some to consider buying at a discount from someone who is behind on their payment or someone who needs to move quickly due to a job or for health reasons. I am by no means advocating taking advantage of anyone. You should never lie or try to con someone into doing something they don't want to do. However, I can assure you that after working with several of these motivated clients as their real estate agent and representative, it's not taking advantage of them if their situation is such that they need a quick sale. Often, a quick sale is more important to them than the amount of money they make. And if the home needs repair, often an "as is" purchase is important to them. They can't afford to make repairs. Someone looking to buy a home to live in is not typically drawn to homes like that, and no one is going to offer them top dollar "as is" when the house is in bad condition. As an investor, you buying the home from them is the answer they've been looking for and takes a lot of stress and pressure off of them.

On numerous occasions, I've met with sellers who had thousands of dollars in equity but were in financial trouble. My real estate brokerage listed their home as their representative, meaning my team and I were working for them. And if they confide in me that if they don't sell their house in the next four weeks, it will be foreclosed on and they will lose it all, an investor buyer is their best solution. In that situation, I need to find a buyer for their home quickly. Even if they sell it for less than full market price, it's a win for them. Selling a few thousand dollars below market but putting cash in their bank account is better than a foreclosure on their credit and no cash in the bank.

Cases like this don't happen frequently, but they happen and sellers are ecstatic when we can make a sale happen. Often, it takes an investor to make it happen. If you can be that investor, you are not taking advantage of them. You are saving them from foreclosure.

OUT OF THE SMOG, JUST IN TIME, AN EXAMPLE STORY

Let me tell you a true story. I met with a gentleman and his son who were living in a condo that he had inherited from his mother free and clear with no mortgage. Both father and son had recently lost their jobs. They both smoked in the condo, so it reeked of cigarette smoke. It was so bad that when you took a picture off the wall, you could see its outline. There was that much tar on the walls! The carpet was old. Overall, it was not in great shape. This unit would not be attractive to most buyers, especially to live in.

The gentleman informed me that he had taken out a small home equity line of credit against the condo and could no longer make the payments to the bank since both he and his son had lost their jobs. He had only borrowed around $20K but would lose the condo soon to foreclosure if it was not sold. I listed it for them. If the condo had been in great shape, at the time it would have been worth around $110K. We sold it to a cash buyer for $80K. The buyer got a good deal but also a big job to do! The seller walked away with a chunk of cash. If we had not worked out that deal, he would have lost the home and the $60K that he walked away with! A $60K check handed to a man who is currently unemployed is an answer to his prayers. In this situation, it was a win for the buyer and for the seller. And, I earned a little commission. It was truly a win-win. That is what I always shoot for in my business dealings.

EXITING A HEFTY NEST, AN EXAMPLE STORY

This is another true story. I was involved in another sale where the individual did not want to list his house, but simply wanted me to find a buyer to bring him an offer. He was a hoarder. There was a path through the house with boxes, papers, and just stuff stacked and piled in every room. There were bills and mail on the tables and counters with dates on them from 5 to 6 years prior. Obviously, there is no way to list that house on the open market. There would be no way to make the pictures look good online and no way to even really show it to prospective buyers because he didn't want to clean it out or have showings. This individual was not in great health, and he desired to move back to another state where he had lived when he was younger. In fact, he talked to me while sitting in his bed with a stack of stuff all around him. It resembled somewhat of a nest. He would chain smoke cigarettes and drink soda as we talked.

He didn't have much money, but he did have equity in his house. It was in a great location. He had met with and asked another agent that was a neighbor and friend of his to help him sell it and move. She had been unsuccessful in bringing him an offer.

This house was in a desirable part of town, but needed a ton of work and obviously could not be marketed on the open market as you could hardly walk through it. Plus, he told me he didn't want random people walking through it, and he didn't want to leave for showings.

So, I brought one of our investor clients to look at it. This investor made him what I feel was a fair offer in regards to price based on it's condition, but also offered to hire movers and a truck to get him to his new place. It was acceptable to the seller. It was enough to get him a comparable place in the state he was moving to, and it got him to his goal. He was thrilled that as a bonus, he didn't even have to coordinate his own move.

So, yes, he could have cleaned up the house, allowed us to market it and show it, and possibly sold it for more. However, he didn't want the highest possible price. He wanted convenience, and that's what he got.

The buyer completely gutted and remodeled the house, added some square footage and sold it for a profit. This too was a win-win for all parties involved.

Deals and motivated sellers with unique situations are out there. You've just got to find them, and sometimes you need a top real estate agent or team to help you. Not all agents know how to find these deals, but the good ones do.

THE NEED FOR SPEED, ANOTHER EXAMPLE

In another instance, I actually bought a property from a gentleman and his wife who wanted to move quickly. He contacted me about listing their house and representing them to sell it for a commission. As a real estate broker, this is my primary business.

He said they were moving to another state to be closer to family and needed to sell quickly. After reviewing sales in their neighborhood, I showed them that they could likely sell it for around $90,000 as is. He quickly exclaimed, "I don't need to sell it for that much! I only need $65,000." I replied and explained that it was worth more than that. He replied, "I don't care. I don't need that much. I just want to sell it quickly." He also mentioned that they needed to figure out how to get rid of some of the personal items and furniture that they didn't want to take with them.

Again, I explained that it was worth more than $65,000 and that I was certain I could get more for them. He again insisted that he didn't care. So, I finally asked, "What's more important to you—price or speed?" He immediately exclaimed, "Speed!" So, I myself made them an offer to purchase and told them that they could pick their closing date and leave behind anything they didn't need. They were thrilled. His exact words were "That would be great!" And they accepted my offer.

So, I did the honorable thing in that situation by making sure they understood that their house was worth more than they were selling it for. His wife was involved in the conversation as well, and they were both of sound mind. But, in this situation, they didn't care about the money. They wanted to move fast and wanted a quick and easy solution. I gave them what they wanted, and they literally were thrilled.

I never learned why they needed to move so fast. They were moving to another state to be closer to their kids and grandkids. My only guess is that perhaps one of them had a health issue and time with their family was more important to them than getting more money from the sale.

I was happy that I was able to help them and also happy that I was able to get a great deal with equity. This situation was also a win-win. So, the deals are there! You just need to find them or find a great agent to help you find them. And never take advantage of anyone, but seek to find a win-win. It's actually one of the core values of my brokerage and we've seen lots of success by operating this way.

In a buyer's market it's easier to find deals and discounts. In a seller's market, it becomes more difficult; however, deals are available in all markets. You've just got to find them. Often you can find them through a top real estate agent or through other investors. Note that I said a *top* real estate agent. You want to find a mover and a shaker, an agent or team that's doing a lot of transactions. Those are the ones that are most likely to know of the deals.

It's easy to get a real estate license, so there are a lot of agents out there who only do a handful of deals each year and, quite honestly, won't provide a lot of value to you. Take the extra effort and time to find a top-producing agent or team to come alongside of you in your investment business. Find the right one, and let it be a long-term growing relationship. The top producers can identify the deals if deals are on the market, and they also often know of off-market deals that may not be publicly advertised. Go to www.TheRealEstateWayBook .com/findagent to find our recommendations for a top real estate agent in your area.

FINDING DEALS AND BUYING: A NUTSHELL

Motivated sellers are the best sellers. They are the ones who will give favorable pricing and terms. Look for those opportunities.

However, **don't spend all your time looking for that "deal of a lifetime" and never take action!** When investing in a rental property, you also want to consider your rate of return (remember, from chapter 5?). Run the numbers, and if they make sense, do the deal! To assist you, download the free Rental Property ROI Tool by going to www.TheRealEstateWayBook.com/gift. Again, my recommendation is to invest for cash flow from rents. Don't invest for appreciation. Consider appreciation a bonus if you get it. But, buy where you expect appreciation when you can. It can be huge, and you can see windfalls when a property appreciates. Just don't speculate.

If you always buy for cash flow from rental income, you can't go wrong. If you are getting enough money each month to cover a mortgage payment, repairs, and expenses, and you have some left over, you shouldn't lose (unless you are just foolish with managing your money or the property). The monthly cash will get you through. And most of the time, if you select properties correctly, you will see appreciation. The more homes you own that appreciate, the more your wealth will grow!

As long as you invest for your required rate of return, you should get it year after year until you sell the asset. Furthermore, the return should only increase year over year as rents rise. Even with no appreciation in the home's value, if you are getting a nice return on your investment, it's worth it. In my opinion, it's certainly better than the stock market, risky commodities, or currency trading. You get the rate of return you need, AND you still own the entire asset. Another win-win!

In the next two chapters, we'll talk about how to pay for the deal when you find that motivated seller or that deal that has the equity and ROI you are looking for.

CHAPTER 7
Funding Deals: Part 1—Going Traditional

In the next two chapters, we'll look at options for funding the purchase of real estate. This chapter outlines the traditional and simplest ways to fund a purchase. These methods require you to have some money on hand in order to buy outright or for a down payment if getting a loan, and you will need to have a good credit score.

The next chapter includes ways to be creative and methods you can use if you don't have cash in your bank account or good credit. I'm sure you've seen the infomercials about buying real estate with "no money down." It can be done, but it's much more complicated and difficult than the traditional methods. And, as you'll learn in chapter 8, it's not quite as easy as they make it sound on their ads.

After reading the following two chapters, you'll likely lean in one direction or another, depending on your unique situation. No matter which way you lean you must have a plan and a way to acquire properties before you can start making offers. You know your financial situation. So, after learning the different methods in these two chapters, you can develop a plan. The point is—have a plan! The last thing you want to do is go under contract on a property and then default because you can't get to the closing table. Unfortunately, as a real estate broker, I've seen this happen too. Buyers get overly ambitious and then can't close due to lack of funding, so they sometimes lose earnest money. This and the next chapter will help you get your funding in order.

TRADITIONAL METHODS FOR FUNDING REAL ESTATE

The methods in this chapter describe the traditional ways of funding real estate, like paying cash or using institutional financing. If you've saved a little money to invest, this can be a great way to start because it's easy, you can make solid offers, and you are not dependent upon anyone other than yourself.

I prefer and recommend that my clients buy investment properties either with cash, a line of credit, or institutional financing with 20% down. These are just the easiest ways to do it if you have funds available from those sources. This is how I typically buy properties as well. Because I like to buy homes below market when I can, an offer that's cash or has solid financing will be more attractive to the seller. Sometimes I'll refinance those properties to leverage them to buy others, and we'll discuss that as well.

Let's look at a few of these methods.

THE CASH PURCHASE

A cash purchase can be an advantageous way to buy because sellers like it. If you were a motivated seller, wouldn't you like to hear, "I'll buy your house with cash and close in two weeks!"? Yes, you would, and motivated sellers love it.

I've actually seen sellers and banks that own repossessed property accept a lower price for a cash deal as opposed to one that has financing involved. Cash just makes it clean and easy, and it's music to a motivated seller's ears. It gives the seller peace of mind knowing that their contract should close and won't fall through due to financing. And when you close, you own it 100%. The bank can't foreclose because there is no debt on the property. Paying cash is also the most conservative way to buy rental property and the simplest.

The problem is not everyone has enough cash on hand to make an entire real estate purchase. However, if you follow the guidelines I give in this book, your wealth will grow and in a few years, you may be making cash offers!

Let's say you do have enough cash to purchase only one property. That's an option. You can do that and collect rent for a few years until you stack up enough cash to buy another. Then you pay cash for this next one. Then, you have twice as much money coming in each month, so in half the time, you can stack cash and buy another. Then you have three times the rent coming in. Rinse and repeat. Make sense?

Consider this example:

Purchase one property for $150,000.

Rent is $18,000 per year.

Cash flow (net income) after expenses = $14,000 per year.

- To buy another house for $150,000, you could do so in 11 years from the $14,000 per year ($14,000 * 11 = $154,000).
- Then you have $28,000 net income per year from two houses, so you could buy another house for $150,000 in 5 to 6 years.
- Then you have $42,000 net income per year from three houses, so you could buy another house for $150,000 in less than 4 years!
- Then you have $56,000 net income per year from four houses, so you could buy another house for $150,000 in less than 3 years!
- Then you have $70,000 net income per year from five houses, so you could buy another house for $150,000 in just over 2 years!
- And so on.

Eventually, you could buy a house every year. Or you could stop buying them, stop working, and simply live off of the income they generate.

Again, this is just an example. The numbers are never going to work out that perfectly. Some years will be better and some worse, but it gives an example of one strategy. This is one option. It's safe and it works, but it can take many years to build a large portfolio. There are better ways!

THE INFINITE RETURN: CASH-OUT REFINANCE METHOD

Another option is to buy the first house with cash. And if you buy it 20% or 30% below market, then after a year, sometimes sooner, you can go to the bank and do what's called a cash-out refinance where you place a mortgage on the property. You can pull out your entire original investment and sometimes more. When you do this, you have all of your money back, so you in essence have created an infinite return on your investment because you no longer have your cash in the deal.

For this option to work, a couple of things will need to happen. First, you will need to own the house for at least one year before you can do a cash-out refinance. Some lenders might do it after 6 months, but most require a year. Some might require longer. Second, the property will need to appraise for the higher amount. The banks typically will only allow you to pull out 80% of the appraised value. So, it will need to appraise for 25% more than your purchasing price if you want to get all of your investment back.

What you are doing is trading your cash for debt. So, now you have a mortgage payment that you did not have before. But, the tenant pays rent, which will service the debt. The leftover cash is your cash flow and your profit, and that is your infinite return. Then you can take the cash you pulled out to go and buy another property.

THE GLORIOUS INFINITE RETURN, AN EXAMPLE

Let's say you purchase a house for $100K, and it rents for $1,000 per month. Either because you bought it at a great price or the market has appreciated, you decide to cash out with a refinance so that you can buy another house. Or, maybe you just want your money back. As long as the house will appraise for $125K, then you can get a loan for $100K. You keep that money and do whatever you like with those funds. I would suggest using it to buy more real estate.

Once you do this, you also have a mortgage payment that you didn't have before. Let's say you finance it for 30 years at a 5% interest rate, then your payment would be $537 per month. Even after taxes, insurance, and repairs, the property should still cash flow (assuming it's a good property). Let's assume it rents for $1,000 per month and that you cash flow $200 per month after all expenses including the mortgage payment. In this case you are getting an infinite return on your investment. You are returning $2,400 per year on essentially a $0 investment because you pulled it back out. You made the $100K investment for one year, then got it back, and it makes a return year after year after year. You will get paid from this property every year. What other investment gives you an infinite return? Not 10%, not 100%, not 1,000%, but an infinite return.

Original investment = $100,000

Original loan amount = $0

New loan amount = $100,000

You have your original investment of $100,000 back.

- Any cash flow on this deal is an infinite return on your investment.

You can do this over and over. This is how people grow a portfolio to 20, 30, or 100 homes in a few years. And when you add in the added bonus of appreciation, tax deductions, and principle pay down, this kind of deal just gets better and better.

My example was based on a cash purchase, but if the equity is there, you can also refinance to wipe out the first mortgage, obtain a larger mortgage, and still pull your original down payment back out and have an infinite return. It works the same way.

The HELOC Method

Another option that is similar to a cash-out refinance, is obtaining a home equity line of credit or HELOC. You can simply ask the bank for a line of credit where the bank will allow you to draw up to 75%-80% of the value against the property. Then, you are essentially leveraging this house, pulling your original investment back out, and you can go purchase another property. HELOCs are typically interest only, and you draw on them like you would a bank account. If you aren't using the money, then you don't pay interest. You only pay when you've made a draw.

The nice thing about a line of credit is that you only pay interest when you use the money, but it's always available just like money in the bank. And it will be available until something crazy happens in the economy and the bank puts a freeze on it, or something like that. That's not likely to happen, so personally, I like the idea of a line of credit. I use lines of credit sometimes to buy houses that I may want to flip. And sometimes I use them to make cash offers and close on a deal, and then I'll take out a mortgage in a few months or the next year to pay down the line of credit. Again, when I buy homes below market value or homes that appreciate, I can get a mortgage and pay back the line of credit, and the cash flow creates that infinite return.

Lines of credit can be placed against existing investment properties that you own or against your primary residence. If your home is currently paid for, a HELOC using your existing house might be a great way to make the equity in your current house work for you to acquire rental properties. Use the HELOC to purchase the rental and then take a mortgage on it to bring your HELOC back to zero.

ON LEVERAGING

You can acquire more properties by leveraging one property to buy another one. Furthermore, if the homes are appreciating in value, then your net worth grows much faster because you have more homes appreciating. If you have two homes worth $100K each, and they appreciate at 4%, then you have gained $8,000 in net worth ($200,000 * 4%). However, if you have 20 homes, each worth $100K, and they all appreciate at 4%, then your net worth has gone up to $80K (20 * $100,000 * 4%).

On the flip side, this can also work in reverse. If values go down 4%, then you lose more wealth if you own more properties. So, the more you leverage, the more exposure and risk you have, so you need to find the balance that's right for you. Again, it's only a gain or loss of net worth on paper, on your balance sheet. You only truly gain or lose when you sell. So as long as you are collecting rent and cash flowing, and don't sell in a down market, then you won't really lose anything. It's not a real loss until you actually complete a transaction and make it a real loss.

TRADITIONAL FINANCING METHOD

Another traditional way to buy that's an alternative to paying cash for one property (if you have funds to pay cash for only one) would also be to put 20% down and buy four or five properties at one time.

You must keep in mind that anytime you use leverage or borrow money from the bank, that debt must be serviced. That means your cash flow on each property is going to decrease. Cumulative cash flow against all properties should be equal to or more than your cash flow on one property.

For example, if you own a house that leases for $1,200 per month and you own it free and clear, you are probably netting around $850 per month ($10,200 per year) after you pay taxes, insurance, repairs, and management. If you refinance or borrow against that property, let's say your debt service is $600 per month. (It will vary depending on how much you borrow.) So, now your cash flow is only $250 per month. But, again, if you pulled out your original cash, then your $250 each month ($3,000 per year) is an infinite return on the original investment.

It works as long as you take that cash, buy another property, and continue to grow your portfolio. If you buy another property with it and add another $1,200 in rent, then you are again cash flowing the original $850 on the second property you purchased, plus the $250 from the first house. Then you repeat this process. Eventually, you'll own multiple properties all cash flowing around $250 per month.

Using this process, you can buy 10, 20, 50, or more properties with leverage in just a few years. Now, when you leverage, you are increasing your risk and exposure, so I'll caution you against overleveraging. At some point, you want to either start paying properties off or selling a few to pay off others. One idea is to grow your portfolio to twice as many houses as you want to end with, then sell off half to pay off the other half after a few years.

When you are young, you can afford to leverage more because if things go south, you have more time to recover. As you get older, you should move to a more conservative approach. However, at any age, as long as you don't overleverage, you should be OK in the long run. As many can attest, when you overleverage, you can lose it all as many did back in 2009 to 2011.

When I say overleverage, what I mean by that is buying a property where there is no or very little cash flow. As long as the mortgage payment is around 50% to 60% of the rent amount, you should be in good shape. You are then left with enough to pay the taxes, insurance, repairs, and property management, and still put money in the bank each month.

BAD ADVICE!

Believe it or not, I've even heard and read where clients are advised that it's OK to buy a property even if there is negative cash flow, which means the owner must contribute money each month in addition to rent in order to cover the mortgage and other expenses. They say you should consider it a contribution, just like you would contribute to a retirement account. Then you wait on the house to appreciate. You will never hear such lousy advice from me! That is a recipe for disaster, and it's why people lose rental houses to foreclosure.

Do not, and I repeat, do not buy a house as an investment that does not or will not cash flow and put positive cash in your bank each month. As I've already stated, buy for cash flow and ROI, not appreciation. Let appreciation be a bonus. In my opinion, buying a rental house where you are required to add money to the rent received in order to pay the mortgage is a BAD investment. At that point, it's a liability.

I get the logic behind it. Since you are contributing to an IRA or a 401K, what's the difference? Why not contribute to real estate? But, that's the beauty of real estate. Someone else contributes it for you! As a general rule, I'd recommend you get rid of properties with negative cash flow unless you are convinced without a shadow of a doubt that you will make it up later through appreciation. Then again, that makes it more like gambling and doesn't really make real estate any more attractive than the stock market.

I like to maintain at least 30% equity in my properties at all times, and I like to have a large margin of cash flow. That way, if the market tanks, I can at least get out or sell a few if I absolutely have to and not lose everything. This is only if I get in a tight spot and need a back-up plan. It would be a very rare instance for me to sell. The smart thing to do is to continue renting and receiving income during a downturn. Focus on increasing your cash flow each month.

My goal in future years is to own several properties and be debt-free. Then, I'm seeing the full amount of cash flow from rent coming in with no risk of losing the properties as long as I pay the taxes. However, the proper use of debt allows me to get there faster.

Two Basic Loan Types

There are two types of loans that are both institutional financing that you can use to purchase real estate. One is what you would consider a traditional mortgage that's backed by Fannie Mae or Freddie Mac. The second is a loan with a local bank.

LONG-TERM LOAN, FANNIE MAE OR FREDDY MAC THROUGH A MORTGAGE LENDER

This is probably the type of loan you used to purchase your primary residence. You go to your local mortgage lender and borrow 80% of the purchase at a fixed interest rate for 30 years. On a primary residence, you can borrow up to 100% of the purchase price with some loan programs. However, for investment property, the lender will require at least 20% down.

You also must own these in your own personal name, and currently you are limited to buying only ten properties with long-term fixed-rate financing that's backed by Fannie Mae or Freddie Mac. If you own the property in a company name or LLC, this type of financing is not an option. Financing properties this way with a long-term fixed-rate loan is best for properties that you intend to hold for many years. If you plan to refinance, pay it off, or sell in a few years, this is not my recommended way.

SHORT-TERM LOAN, IN-HOUSE LOAN WITH A LOCAL BANK

If you plan to sell in a few years or refinance in a few years, or if you own the property in an LLC or company name, I recommend going with a local bank. Your local commercial lender will also loan you 80%. Occasionally, they will loan 85% or possibly 90%, but most will be 80%. Their interest rate may be a little higher than the 30-year fixed-rate. This local bank rate will only be locked for 3 to 5 years, and the loan is typically amortized over 20 years instead of 30. Amortization is the length of time it takes to pay off the loan. Due to a potentially higher interest rate and a shorter amortization, your payment will be higher than with a long-term loan, which means your monthly cash flow will be less. However, the closing costs when you purchase will also be less than half the cost of a long-term mortgage. For these reasons, if you plan to refinance or sell it within 3 to 5 years, in my opinion, this could be a better way to go.

Some people will purchase in their personal name with long-term fixed-rate financing and then transfer the property to an LLC. This is one option, and I've seen it done several times. However, it's possible that you trigger the lender's "due on sale" clause, which would mean the lender could call the entire balance due in full because you transferred the property to another party. However, from my experience, most will not call the loan due as long as they are getting their payment each month. While this is an option, I can't recommend it because it could leave you in a bad spot if the loan is called due. So, exercise this option only at your own risk.

This chapter outlined traditional ways you could go about funding your real estate deal. But these traditional avenues aren't open to everyone. In the next chapter, we'll look at some alternative funding methods so that all readers have options for pursuing financial freedom through real estate investing.

CHAPTER 8
Funding Deals: Part 2—Going Alternative

So, what do you do if you don't have 20% to put down to get started? In order to utilize traditional financing, you must have the down payment. So how can you obtain it?

One option would be to save it by cutting your expenses, getting another job, or finding a side hustle. Since you are looking into real estate, another option would be to find a house to flip to make $25K to $50K. This can also be risky if you underestimate repairs or overestimate the final sales price. If you go this route, make sure you know the market well and have a very knowledgeable real estate agent to guide you.

You'll typically need some money as a down payment in order to flip a house too, so you will still be stuck unless you are able to find a bank or partner who will loan you 100%. It's possible, so don't lose hope. In this chapter, we'll explore options for buying real estate when you don't have money for a down payment.

We've already discussed that you'll need a reserve account in addition to your purchase money or your down payment money when you begin to buy and hold real estate. Buying and holding truly is the way to build wealth long term. It sets you up to receive payments every single month from your tenants for as long as you own the property.

Let's consider a few options for building an investment portfolio with little or no money down.

THE MOVING METHOD

In my opinion, one of the best ways to start is with the "moving" strategy. Earlier I mentioned that banks will loan up to 100% financing in some cases for primary residences. One strategy is that you buy a house to live in, then move every few years, and make the house you moved out of a rental property. Then, you can buy your next primary residence with 95% or 100% financing. And because you are buying it as your primary residence, you'll also get a better interest rate than if you were buying an investment property. This is just one strategy that some people have been successful using.

Of course, you could also sell your primary residence and use the proceeds from the sale for a down payment on a rental property.

One disadvantage to this strategy is that you have to keep moving! You also want to consider that when selling a primary residence that you have lived in for 2 out of the past 5 years, then you can take the profit tax-free. So, in some cases, that might make more sense than keeping it to rent long term. If you don't like this strategy, there are other options.

FUNDING OPTIONS FOR FLIPPING

Many investors get their start by "flipping" a few houses to generate the cash for their down payment and reserve fund.

So, how do you get the funds to flip a house? If you don't have a down payment or can't get a loan from a local bank, there are two options that I recommend. One is what's called a hard money loan. The other is to find a partner that has money. You'll have to figure out what's the best route for you and your situation.

OPTION 1—HARD MONEY

There are hard money lenders that will make loans against the property regardless of whether or not you have money to put down and regardless of your credit. Sound too good to be true? Well, it's true. These lenders will do it, but they may charge anywhere from 12% to 20% interest. They are taking a greater risk, so it's offset by a higher interest rate.

This is why I don't recommend hard money for long-term rental property. However, for the quick flip where you get in and get out in just a few months or weeks, hard money can make sense. The other difficult thing about making hard money loans work is finding the deals that fall within the ratios that hard money lenders require. These hard money lenders are looking at the deal. They are putting their money on the house, and not you. So, if they don't like the deal, they won't make the loan. Hard money lenders will typically loan you about 60% to 70% of the after-repair value of the home.

Here is an example of how hard money might work. I'm using round numbers, so that you can easily see the percentages and break down. These figures may be realistic for your area, or they may not. The important thing is that you use the ratios and percentages, which can be applicable in any market.

Hard Money Example: say you find a deal that you can purchase for $90K. It needs $40K worth of repairs, but when it's complete, it would be worth $200K. You need $130K to purchase and repair the home. Because $130K is 65% of the end value, the hard money lender would finance it for you if they like the property.

Then you would pay interest, either monthly or quarterly, on the $130K that you borrow. That means you would be paying them $1,300 per month at 12% interest or $2,166 per month at 20% interest. This loan is typically due in full in 6 months or a year, which means you will either need to sell it or refinance it within the specified timeframe. The term and rate is something that you would work out with the lender prior to borrowing the money. Rates and terms will vary between lenders.

At these rates, you can see why you want to get in and out fast. The longer it takes to sell the property, the more interest you pay, and the less profit you make. If you don't make the periodic interest payments or if you haven't sold the house by the end of the loan term, the lender can take the property. Then, they make the profit on the house, rather than you.

Even still, in this type of situation, you have the potential of making $60K to $70K, depending on your carrying costs and how long you keep it. That's enough to make a down payment on a house (or possibly two) that you want to keep as a long-term rental. If you prefer to keep the home you've been repairing as a rental, your local bank may refinance it as long as it appraises high enough that your loan payoff is less than 80%.

OPTION 2—PARTNERING

If you don't like the sound of a hard money loan, the other option would be to find a partner. I'm sure you know people in town that have money. Think about business owners, doctors, dentists, etc. Some of these people like the idea of investing in real estate, but they don't have the time to look for deals because their time is very valuable due to the nature of their work. They also like to see their money grow.

If you can offer them a solution where they partner with you on a deal, they provide the money, and their money grows at the end of it, you'll get their attention. There are a few ways a deal could be structured with a partner, and it really is up to you to find a structure that is a win-win for everyone.

It could be structured similar to the hard money loan, but you might be able to convince them to do it at a lower interest rate and with less fees. If they would go for it, great.

The other option would be that you literally partner and decide how to split the profits. They provide the money and you provide all of the work. You might split it 50:50, or it could be some other arrangement. Again, it's whatever you can negotiate and what you both see as a win-win.

An Example of Partnering: let's take the same example we used previously. You are buying a house for $90K and spending $40K to repair it. After you are done, you can sell it for $200K. You might approach a partner with this deal and say, "If you provide the money, I'll do everything else and we'll split the profits evenly."

In this situation, you have no money and no risk in the deal. Your partner is taking the risk. You are doing the work. So, when it sells, let's say the profit is $70K, you would each get $35K. It's a win for you because you just made $35K! You did the work, but you had no money in it and no risk. It's a win for the partner because they just made almost 27% on their money. And if you sell it in 6 months or so, that's an excellent return for them. It's a better return than they can get most other places, and it was completely passive for them. They simply provided the money, and you did the work. With this kind of return, they may want to do more deals with you in the future. Do you see how this can be a win for you both?

Once you do this for them one time, they'll be excited to do another deal with you. You can continue repeating this process until you have enough money to start investing long term. Then you can choose to strike out on your own or continue the partnership.

You can also structure more complicated partnerships where the money partner gets the first payout and then the remaining profits are split at a different percentage. The investor's initial payout could be a flat rate or a certain percentage.

Another Partnering Example: you could structure it so the investor gets the first $20K from the sale and then the remaining profit is split at 20% to them and 80% to you. This ensures the partner a certain return. In this case, the investor is ensured a 15% return even if you make nothing. The money partner has some assurance that if your sale projection is too high and you can only sell the house for $160K, instead of $200K, they still get their money back and make their return. Your profit is on the back end. This makes the money partner feel safer about making the investment.

In the above scenario, if you sold the house for $200K, making $70K total profit, the money partner would get $20,000 + $10,000 (20% of $50,000) = $30,000. You would get $40K. If you overestimated what you could sell the house for and it only sold for $160K and made $30K total profit, the investor would get $20,000 + $2,000 (20% of $10,000) = $22,000, and you would only get $8,000 (80% of the $10,000). So a structure like this gives the money partner less risk, but also makes it much more profitable to you if you are able to perform at a high level and make more profit on the deal.

Some partners may not go for a split as outlined above. Since they have the cash, they have the control. The investor partner may want a preferred rate upfront and then want a 50/50 split with you since they are taking all of the monetary risk.

There is probably an infinite number of ways deals can be structured with partners. At the end of the day, it just has to be a structure you can both agree on and that you both feel is fair. These are just a couple of examples to get you thinking.

Just like the hard money loan, the partner will want a structure where if the property isn't sold in a certain amount of time or if you haven't paid them a certain amount of money by a certain time, they can take 100% ownership of the property. And that's fair. After all, it's all their money invested in it.

NOTE: I'll be honest with you. The biggest problem with the above scenario is finding the deals that can be bought with this much equity. It's hard to do! Not impossible, but difficult. But, I needed to use that illustration to show you how hard money works. So, while you may hear about hard money and how it's a great way to do real estate deals, that's only partially true. It is a great way to fund deals where there is a lot of equity. The problem is finding that much equity. In recent years, as more and more investors compete for deals, 75% to 85% tends to be more realistic than 65%. Many hard money lenders won't loan that much of the value. With a partner, it may not matter as much as long as you both agree with the projected profit and agree on how it is paid out.

Partnering over the Long Term: you can also set up similar partnership structures for holding rental property long term as well. However, I would advise you to use caution when entering partnerships on long-term deals. I like them for quick deals where you get in and out, and all parties know the plan.

In my experience, for investments that you hold for many years with a partner, there can be problems. A lot of things can change over a period of several years. What happens if one partner wants to sell and the other doesn't? Or what happens if one partner gets into financial trouble? Or what happens if one partner wants to spend a large amount of money to improve a property and the other doesn't? There are just too many things that can go wrong over a long period of time. Don't get me wrong. Some partnerships work great and the partners complement each other very well whereas others have ruined great friendships. The exit strategies need to be agreed upon prior to forming the partnership, but the longer it continues, the greater the chances of something not working out.

Long-term partnerships work great for a lot of people, and this may be a route you want to take. For me, personally, I typically only like partnerships on shorter projects with a clear plan.

OPTION 3—OWNER FINANCING

The last form of creative financing I want to mention is owner financing. This is not a likely scenario as you would be forced to find a seller who didn't have a mortgage and who would be willing to sell to you and receive payment each month rather than a lump sum. Most motivated sellers want a lump sum, not a small payment each month.

So, while this is an option and something for you to consider and have in your tool belt, it's not likely something you'll encounter very often. I see more situations where real estate investors will offer owner financing to individuals with a goal of maximizing their return. If they are trying to maximize their return, it's probably not going to be a great deal for you. So, it's not likely that you will find a below market deal AND owner financing. Usually it's one or the other.

Take some time now to consider where you are financially and what options seem the most practical for you. The kinds of deals you can find and the amount of equity will have some bearing on your options. For you, will it be traditional financing or an alternative method? If you go alternative, will you find a partner or get a hard money loan? This answer will be different for everyone.

Again, the easiest and most efficient way for you to begin acquiring properties is with traditional financing. Next would be with a partner. The most difficult is hard money simply because it's hard to find the deals with equity that fit their requirements. When you do find the equity, you'll likely encounter competition with other investors that are using traditional financing or paying cash. So, I recommend using traditional methods if possible. If you don't have the cash, finding a money partner is the next best option.

By either traditional or alternative routes, once you've lined up the money and moved on the deal, you'll have to decide the best way to hold title. That's what the next chapter is about.

CHAPTER 9
Holding Title

Once you begin acquiring real estate, you'll want to take into consideration how you will hold title. That is, in what name will the property be held?

In this chapter, we'll consider the most common options for holding real estate titles:

- Personally as an Individual

- Tenants in Common

- Joint Tenants with Right of Survivorship

- Limited Liability Company

- Trust

As you'll learn, there are pros and cons for each, depending on your situation and goals.

Many people simply take title in their personal names, and that's fine. Sometimes they title it in their name and add a spouse. That's how most people take title to their personal homes. It's often in both spouses' names. Sometimes it's only in one spouse's name if that's the one that qualified for the mortgage. However, often you see them both on title jointly. This makes sense because in most families both are contributing to the mortgage payment, and if not, they still see themselves as one unit.

When taking ownership individually with another person, there are two ways this can be done. It may be different in other states, but in Georgia, there are two ways: tenants in common (TIC) and joint tenants with right of survivorship.

TENANTS IN COMMON

With tenants in common (TIC), each individual named on the title has equal rights to the property. They have 50/50 ownership. They literally each own half of the property. If one dies, then their half will be distributed down through their estate according to their will.

When partnering with someone other than a spouse, most often, you want to hold title as tenants in common. This way, your heirs will still have the ownership of half of the property upon your death. I also see spouses title property this way if they are older, on their second marriage, and their preference is that their ownership rights would go to their children rather than the surviving spouse.

JOINT TENANTS WITH RIGHT OF SURVIVORSHIP

Because of the structure of TIC, it can be problematic if two people hold title as tenants in common if their intentions are for 100% of it to go to the surviving person upon the death of one. With the second type of ownership, joint tenants with right of survivorship, this solves that problem. With this type of tenancy, the property automatically goes directly to the surviving partner and does not flow down through the estate. It does not even need to go through probate but automatically goes 100% to the surviving partner. This is the most common type of tenancy used by married couples.

I recommend you speak with an attorney or an accountant that is an expert in this area if you intend to hold property with a partner, whether it be a spouse, family member, or a friend.

LIMITED LIABILITY COMPANY

Another common way to hold title to real estate is through a limited liability company or LLC. By setting up an LLC, it provides you some level of anonymity and also creates a separate entity to hold the real estate. When set up properly, it can give you some level of protection from lawsuits, etc. Basically, you don't own the house. The LLC owns the house. And you just own the LLC. There are ways good attorneys can pierce through this structure, so it's not bulletproof, but my understanding is that it does add a layer of protection.

An LLC is somewhat simple to set up. It requires filing paperwork with the state and registering the name of the company. You can do this yourself, but I recommend you use an attorney or a qualified accountant.

The LLC can be formed as a single-member LLC, meaning it's just you. Or, it can have several members. If you decide to have partners, sometimes an LLC is a great structure. The LLC operating agreement can spell out the ownership and rights of each of the partners.

You can also write off repairs and maintenance when filing your taxes through the LLC. Technically, you can write off repairs if you own it in your personal name as well, but it's good for accounting reasons to track it all separately. So, even if you don't set up an LLC, I recommend you track your rental expenses and income in a separate checking account.

There are some drawbacks to holding property in the name of an LLC. One is that you can't get conventional long-term financing backed by Fannie Mae or Freddie Mac. Basically, an LLC can't get a 30-year fixed-rate mortgage. Only individuals can. If the LLC is going to borrow money, it can, but you must work through a local bank.

TRUST

Sometimes you'll even see property held in a trust. This is another legal way to hold property that gives some protection to the individual and also provides some privacy. Trusts have been set up for years by wealthy people to create privacy and protect their assets.

Personally, I take the advice of well-respected attorneys and my CPA on how to title property and how to take the biggest advantage of the tax breaks while staying within the law. I like to understand the pros and cons of each. So, I recommend you get advice from your trusted advisors as well.

As it just so happens, I own property both personally and in different LLCs and I've explored trusts. So, there are different strategies in different situations and for different people. Detailed explanations of each advantage and disadvantage is beyond the scope of this book. I just wanted to mention the different types, so you are aware of several options and can seek proper guidance and counsel for your situation. I highly advise you speak with a competent CPA or attorney about the legal structure you choose and the advantages and disadvantages of each.

Just as there are pros and cons to how you title your property, when running your property as a rental or when selling it, there are pros and cons in terms of taxation. To make your real estate investment work for you, it's important to familiarize yourself with real estate-related taxes, the topic of chapter 10.

CHAPTER 10
Harnessing Tax Advantages

Let me start this chapter by restating that I am neither a CPA nor a tax expert, and I recommend you get tax advice from someone other than me. The examples used in this chapter and throughout this book are for illustrative purposes only. I want to take this chapter to explain the tax benefits of owning real estate as I understand them and as I've applied them to my own investments with the help of a CPA. Additionally, we'll consider what happens with taxes when you sell real estate.

TAX DEDUCTIONS ON INTEREST

The first tax advantage to owning real estate is that when financing, the interest is tax deductible. That means if you have a mortgage payment of $700 per month, most of which is interest, and at the end of the year, let's say you have paid $6,000 in interest, then that $6,000 is deductible as an expense.

In the early years of a mortgage, most of the payment is interest, but as time goes on, you begin to pay more principal and less interest. This is one reason some people prefer to refinance their properties rather than sell them or pay them off.

If you pay them off, you lose the interest deduction. If you sell them, you pay capital gains tax and tax on the recaptured depreciation. By refinancing them, you can take cash out tax-free and increase your mortgage interest deduction. On the other hand, you are now paying more out as interest even though it is deductible.

Also, when you do this, you decrease your cash flow because you have a higher payment. And in my opinion, to be completely financially free is to be debt-free.

Each individual will have to find their own plan and strategy that works for them, but take advantage of the tax savings by writing the interest off of your loans if you have them.

TAX DEDUCTIONS ON EXPENSES

Any expenses, such as management expenses, office expenses, and repairs to the property, are also tax deductible. Often, you can even deduct mileage as you travel to check on your properties. Small repairs are deductible in that calendar year whereas capital improvements must be depreciated. We'll get more into depreciation in a minute.

Basically, you can spend money to improve your property making it more valuable, either in small ways or in large ways, and our government allows you to deduct it from your income when it's time to pay taxes. Think about it. You are improving the property you own and enhancing its value with non-taxable dollars.

PROPERTY DEPRECIATION

Another tax benefit is that the property can be depreciated over a period of 27.5 years. That means that you can write off about 3.6% of the house each year through depreciation. This is where you may need to involve your CPA because different parts of the house can be depreciated differently. For example, appliances can typically be depreciated in 5 years, and the land itself is not depreciable at all. For driveways and sidewalks, it's 15 years.

To show the advantages of depreciation, let's take an example. Say you buy a house for $150K, and the land is valued at $25K. That means you can depreciate $125K as the value of the house. That means you can write off $4,545 each year as depreciation. You still receive income on the property, but you won't pay tax on $4,545. You also won't pay tax on the interest and other repairs. Can you see how you can make money with rental property but show a very small income from it for taxes? That's why real estate is a great tax shelter.

When you buy a new appliance, it is depreciated over a period of 5 years. There have been some recent changes to the tax law, and they are constantly changing, so I recommend you defer this to your trusted CPA to work out your depreciation. However, as you can see, there are benefits to using this tax strategy.

Depreciation is like magic in real estate. While the house actually will appreciate in value over time, which means its value will increase, you can depreciate it on your taxes, which means you don't pay taxes on all of the income. Rental property can sometimes work out to show a loss on taxes due to interest, depreciation, management fees, and repairs even though the property does cash flow.

TAX BENEFITS IN COMBO

Let's look again at our example of the $150K property. Say it rents for $1,500 per month. That's $18,000 per year as income to you. However, because it's from real estate, it's taxed differently than if you made that income from your job. Without the tax advantages, you would pay taxes at your tax rate on that $18,000. Think about how much your employer takes out of your paycheck. At a 30% tax rate, on $18,000, your tax owed would be $5,400. It's much less when the income is from renting real estate.

With the tax benefits of deducting interest, real estate taxes, insurance, and depreciation, it could look more like: $18,000 − $6,000 (loan interest) − $600 (insurance) − $1,500 (real estate taxes) − $4,545 (depreciation) = $5,355. Now you would only pay tax on $5,355, which at 30% is $1,607. This amount is less than a third of what you would pay if you were earning that same amount of money with your salary.

The reality is you would also likely have management fees and a few expenses. If your management and placement fees are $1,800, then you would also deduct that. If you had repairs throughout the year of, let's say, $600, then you could also deduct that. Then your taxable income is reduced to $2,955, and your tax at 30% would be $887. So, your tax if you earned $18,000 in salary is $5,400, and with rental real estate with this scenario, it's $887. That's a huge difference.

The reality is that your net income in the above scenario would have been $7,500. So, you pocket $7,500 gross and pay tax of $887. That's a tax rate of less than 12% on the true earnings.

Can you see that by applying these tax strategies you can save in taxes? If you have a property that needs a lot of repair, there may be some years that you show a loss or a breakeven and pay no tax. In the above scenario, we only had an average amount of repairs and we only showed income of $2,955 even though we really made $7,500. This is due to the depreciation and interest deduction that the IRS allows you to take. The goal is not to pay no tax as that typically means you made little or no money. However, the goal is to pay less tax while keeping the property profitable.

And that's also why I recommend you invest in properties that are in good condition and you maintain them. Or if you purchase them in need of repair, make those repairs on the front end. Large repairs can make the difference between a profit and a loss with rental property.

Taxes and Selling Real Estate

You may know that when you sell your primary residence, you can take the gain tax-free as long as you've lived there for 2 of the past 5 years.

However, when you sell an investment property, it's going to be taxed at the capital gains tax rate, which is currently 15% to 20% for the IRS, plus whatever rate your state charges. That means if you sell an investment property that you bought 10 to 15 years ago, and you make $100K profit on it, then you could pay $20K+ in taxes.

In addition, if you remember from the earlier "Property Depreciation" section, you've been depreciating this property to save on taxes. The IRS requires that you recapture the depreciation tax savings you took in previous years, so you will be required to pay it back now. This could be another $25K to $30K that you would owe, depending on how long you've owned the property. In all you could end up paying $45K to $50K in taxes if you sell for $100K profit and you've owned it several years. That's a large tax bill and can sometimes make you think twice about selling.

Because of this, I only recommend selling if you are willing to consider the tax consequence and you need the funds for something else or if you plan to buy another piece of real estate.

A Loophole to Lay Hold Of

When you buy more real estate, there is a loophole and a way to defer paying the tax. That's done through a 1031 tax-deferred exchange. Sometimes it's called a tax-free exchange. While you pay no tax while you participate, it's not technically tax-free. It's tax deferred. That's why the most appropriate term is 1031 tax-deferred exchange. This strategy is 100% legal and can allow you to defer paying the steep capital gains tax we just looked at in the previous section.

There are some rules in order to qualify for a 1031 tax-deferred exchange. The first qualifier is that you have to "exchange" or replace the property that you sold with what the IRS terms as a "like-kind" property. The IRS considers most investment real estate "like-kind" as other investment real estate. You can sell a vacant lot and exchange into another piece of property with a house on it. Or you can sell a house and invest in a duplex or small apartment. Again, these are my interpretations, and I'm not a tax advisor or CPA, so I suggest you contact your tax advisor and get their input and guidance before following my advice.

When you sell the property you plan to exchange, you cannot accept any funds upon the sale. If you do, it will void the exchange. The funds must be sent to a qualified intermediary who will administer the exchange to hold the funds. These funds are typically held in a trust account with the intermediary.

Also, it's important to note that the intermediary cannot be your real estate broker or your closing attorney. It must be an independent agent that has no other part in the transaction. There are companies that specialize in helping clients complete a 1031 exchange, and that's all they do. However, I've had clients work with attorneys and other agents who can hold it and act as the intermediary. It's important that it's done properly so that you get the benefit of deferring the tax and aren't stuck with an unexpected tax bill. If the money gets into your hands or your bank account, it will void the exchange and be very costly to you. So, an independent intermediary must hold it.

The property you sell and the property you buy must both be investment properties. You cannot and would not use the 1031 tax-deferred exchange for a primary residence. You do not actually have to make a trade with someone to exchange properties, and the exchange does not have to be completed on the same day. However, there are some time limits and requirements that you must meet.

The first one is that you must identify the replacement property within 45 days of closing on the first property. This must be done in writing and be provided to your qualified intermediary that is holding your funds.

The next timeline is that the property you are purchasing to exchange for the one you sold must be closed within 180 days from the closing on your sale. If you don't use all of the funds in the exchange, any portion that you receive is subject to tax.

A few other things to consider if you want to defer all of the tax is: (1) you must buy property that is equal to or greater in value than the property you sold. (2) If you have a loan on the property you sold, then you must replace the loan, and any cash that comes from the sale must all go into the new purchase.

When you identify your replacement property, you can identify up to three properties that are similar, or if you are buying lower-priced properties, you can identify more, but the total value of all of them cannot exceed twice the price of the property you sell.

For example, let's say you are selling a property for $200K. You can identify up to three replacement properties that are $200K or more. You can also choose properties that are less, but to get the full tax value, you must spend at least $200K on the next property or combination of properties. The other option is you could buy four properties that are priced at $50K each. And in this case, you could identify up to eight properties at that price range as long as the total price of all of the properties does not exceed $400K because the property you are selling is $200K.

Years down the road, when you sell this new asset you have purchased, you have the option of exchanging it again using the 1031 or selling it straight and receiving the funds. Once you sell and receive the proceeds, that's when you'll be responsible to pay the tax that's due.

The 1031 tax exchange must be reported on your tax return for the same year that you completed the exchange. It's reported on Form 8824. On this form, you'll report relevant information, such as dates, prices, property descriptions, etc.

Again, the 1031 tax exchange is a sophisticated investment strategy. There are pros and cons to it, and I highly recommend you consult with your tax advisor before utilizing this strategy in your business. However, in the right circumstances, it can save you thousands, or at least defer thousands of dollars that you would otherwise be paying in taxes. It can truly be a wealth builder.

TRY TO HOLD ON

I would also like to add that I recommend you don't sell and utilize a 1031 exchange unless you really want to be rid of the property or unless you really have a great property in mind to buy. I almost made the mistake one time of selling a property that had a lot of equity. My eyes got big because I could sell and make a nice profit due to the property values appreciating rapidly in that area. But, after looking at the tax consequences of selling and the lack of available properties to purchase through a tax exchange, I decided it was better to keep it and continue renting it. I had recently replaced the roof, HVAC, and water heater, so I figured it shouldn't require any expensive repairs in the future. The takeaway: I caution you to really analyze your situation and make sure you have a plan before you jump.

Investing in real estate has lots of advantages, one of them being many tax benefits. It can be leveraged with mortgages, it can be depreciated, and taxes can be deferred. I'm not aware of any of these things that can be done with other investments, such as stocks, commodities, or currencies.

You may not think saving or deferring taxes gives you a great advantage, but think about what you can do over a period of years by reinvesting $50K tax savings as opposed to paying it in tax. Fifty thousand dollars invested at just 6% per year is $3,000 per year or $60K over 20 years. Compounded it's a lot more than that. For this reason, I recommend you are knowledgeable of and take advantage of the tax benefits as part of your real estate investment strategy.

Now that you know the tax benefits of owning income-producing property, to really make it perform it must be put into service and managed properly. Then it will actually start making you money. That's what's up next.

CHAPTER 11
Managing Properties

Once you have purchased your first rental property, in order for it to be successful and make you money every month it must be managed properly. Management includes finding and screening tenants, handling security deposits, completing move-in inspections at the time of move-in, collecting rent, periodic inspections, making repairs, and everything in-between. You can do this yourself or hire professional management.

You actually have two assets that you must take good care of when you own real estate. The first one is the property itself. You have a structure on a piece of land, and it has real value. It's an asset because it has value and it's real. And if history repeats itself, it will go up in value over a long period of time if it's well cared for. The second asset is the tenant. Yes, the tenant is an asset to you because without the tenant, you don't get paid every month. You must be intentional about taking good care of both assets!

Remember how earlier we compared owning rental property to that of owning a business? Think of the tenant as the customer at your business. A business won't be a business long if it mistreats its customers. This applies to you as well. Don't think of the tenant as only a tenant but as an asset that must be taken care of. Historically, I think landlords have viewed tenants as having little importance and as "only tenants." They would show little concern for their welfare. Landlords acted as though they could "lord" over the tenants. That's why tenants have historically been mistreated, and landlords have gotten a bad reputation.

What I encourage is that you think of these tenants first and foremost as people. That's what they are. They are people just like you and me, and should be treated as such. Too many landlords don't think this way. In addition, if you want to view it more opportunistically, just remember, when you treat them well, they are more likely to stay, which means your return on investment will be higher in the long run.

In today's world of social media and online reviews, it's more important than ever to maintain a good reputation both offline and online. We now live in a transparent world and word travels quickly. You should do things right and treat people right because it's the right thing to do. But, if that's not enough for you, also consider that your reputation will follow you online. So, selfishly, you should do the right thing, or it will hurt your ability to rent your homes in the future. This also holds true for the property manager, should you choose to hire one. Make sure they are treating tenants properly, and often this is reflected by online reviews as well.

In this chapter, we are going to discuss how to manage the property itself. In the next chapter, we'll talk about how to manage the tenant.

When you own property, just like anything else, there will be required maintenance and repairs. If you own your own home, you know that maintenance and occasional repairs are necessary. If you own a car, you know that maintenance and repairs are necessary. This is true for anything you own. So, don't be surprised when your rental property needs a repair. And don't neglect the routine maintenance that may prevent more costly repairs later. I've personally seen individual owners who self-manage as well as professional managers neglect routine maintenance and it ends up being very costly to the owner in the long run.

Reserve Fund

With this in mind, my first recommendation to anyone who owns real estate is to have a reserve fund. This is money that is set aside separately that is only used for repairs and maintenance to your rental properties. Once you establish this account, it's not a bad idea to set aside a portion of your rent check each month to go into this fund. This way, you don't have to dig into your personal savings account to cover repairs.

Honestly, the amount of repairs that are needed will vary per property depending on the condition of each one. If you have a relatively new house with newer appliances, newer HVAC, newer roof, etc., then your repair and maintenance expenses will be relatively low. If you have an older property and have a major system like HVAC go out, it could take four or five months of rent payments just to cover that one repair.

Those major systems can last up to 30 years, and sometimes they die in 10 years, so there is no way to know. You just need to be prepared.

There is no hard and fast rule of how much money you should have set aside. You should be able to make this determination by thinking of the worst-case scenario and plan accordingly. The routine repairs are going to be for relatively inexpensive things that arise, like small plumbing issues, electrical issues, wood rot. Those can be fixed for a few hundred bucks or less. A tenant may call because a toilet is constantly running, a faucet is dripping, or a breaker is tripping. These are very minor and won't take a major toll on your cash flow.

However, if you have a 20-year-old HVAC or a 20-year-old roof, just know that either will likely need to be replaced in the next few years. They could last another 10 years, or they could go out this year. So, you need to be prepared. And you need to have funds set aside.

The most expensive repairs you will encounter will be replacing the major systems. Normally, they can be patched or repaired at first, but if you are repairing a major system, like the roof or HVAC, multiple times in a short period of time, then the end is near. You need to be ready to replace it soon. It's wasting resources to continue to patch a failing system.

The next major area of repair will be for things like water heaters and appliances. Those also have a life expectancy, so know when the end is drawing near and be prepared.

Otherwise, most of your expenses will come when you are turning over a unit between tenants. This is often when the flooring may need to be replaced, walls may need to be painted, etc., in order to attract a new tenant that is qualified and willing to pay the market rent. Remember that vacancies are a big expense, so you want to limit them. Do all you can to keep the property occupied. If you are missing out on $1,200 per month in rent, then technically, it's a $1,200-per-month expense.

SMALL UPDATES = BIG IMPACT

Sometimes it makes sense to spend a little more money to update kitchens or bathrooms in order to collect more rent. You have to analyze the numbers to see if it makes sense. For example, let's say you own a property free and clear and you are making a 10% return on it. If you could update the kitchen by simply painting cabinets and installing granite at a cost of $4,000, but that would allow you to rent it for $100 more per month, that's a $1,200 return on a $4,000 investment, which is a 30% return. In my opinion, that would be a smart thing to do. You'll collect more rent, and you've improved the property and increased its value for a later resale.

Another improvement that I always recommend for consideration is flooring. If it's time to replace carpet, consider installing a vinyl plank-type product that looks like wood. It will cost more than carpet, but it will enhance the desirability of the home and it will last longer than carpet, meaning you can go longer without needing to replace the flooring again. The vinyl planks may last 3 to 4 times as long as carpet. Some even have 10-or 20-year warranties. Let's say it cost $1,000 more than carpet but will last 3 to 4 times as long, and you can get $100 more per month for rent. That would be a no-brainer. You would get all of your money back in year one and then some. That's more than a 100% return on your investment.

These "wood look" floors are popular in our area at the present time of this writing. It could all be different in 10 to 20 years, and it may be different in other markets. Go with what's attractive and what people like. The same finishes that attract buyers will attract tenants. However, also use some common sense, and if you can use a product that is attractive and more durable and will last longer for just a little bit more money, then do it.

When I replace carpet in my rentals, I'm currently going back with these "wood look" vinyl planks. They are waterproof, pet proof, and look great. And I know when the tenants move, they can be cleaned up easily. There will be no need to hire a professional carpet cleaner or to replace carpet, which will save me money in the long run.

Again, run the numbers to see if it makes sense, but it's these small things that can make a big impact. If you always think in terms of return on investment and do everything you can to maximize that number, your wealth will grow, allowing you to expand, buy more properties, and continue to grow your wealth. In time, it will begin to snowball.

ROUTINE MAINTENANCE

Don't neglect the routine maintenance. It's easy to only look at paper and see a high return on your investment for the year because you had very little expenses because you saved money by not doing necessary maintenance and repairs. However, in the long run, this is a big mistake.

One simple example I can give is cleaning gutters. Water and weather can wreak havoc on a home. I've seen clogged gutters cause all kinds of problems on houses. Gutters being full and clogged can cause water to back up under shingles and cause the roof to leak, which causes roof deck damage outside and sheetrock damage inside. Clogged gutters can also cause water to get into soffits and rot out the soffits and the fascia board.

Most people don't realize it, but many times when homes have moisture issues in the basement or crawl space, it's due to gutters either not being cleaned out or not being extended away from the house. Moisture in the crawl space can lead to mold, mildew, and lots of other costly problems. A good home inspector can explain the importance of clean gutters and getting water away from the house. Repairing these damages will cost a lot more than the annual $100 to $200 or so for routine maintenance. To me, cleaning gutters is just one of those things that should be done annually to protect your investment.

Another example is changing heating and air filters. I have personally experienced this problem and learned the hard way. I replaced a heating and air unit when it was only 6 or 7 years old. The technician explained that the unit failed and died because it was under too much stress due to the filter being completely clogged.

The lease stated that the tenants should replace the filter regularly, but most homeowners don't replace their filters regularly, so how can we expect tenants to do it? When is the last time you changed your HVAC filter in your home? Or your rental homes?

PERIODIC INSPECTIONS

A good practice is to inspect the house and change the air filter regularly. This will extend the life of your unit. It will also allow you the opportunity to walk through and do a visual inspection of the property. If you don't want to inspect the house and change the filter, consider a maintenance contract with a heating and air company. You want to stay in front of problems that may arise, so they don't become more costly later. By inspecting periodically, if something else has started to go wrong, you catch it early.

Let's say a leak has started under the sink or there is a small stain on the ceiling. The tenant may or may not notice it and may or may not notify you. If you are there periodically, you can look for things like this to proactively address before it gets worse.

Finding problems early and remedying them is much better than waiting for a problem to get out of hand.

TURN MINIMIZATION AND MARKET RATE RENT

Also, to properly manage your property, you want to minimize turn. That means you want to minimize how often the property turns over between tenants. If you can keep a tenant in a property for more years, then you spend less on the property.

Turn is costly because the property is sometimes vacant for a period of time, and there are expenses related to cleaning, painting, replacing flooring, etc. Sometimes, it's only a short time, like a week. But, if the property is vacant for a week, on a $1,200 per month rent, that's $300 of lost income.

In the next chapter, we'll discuss more about keeping tenants happy and keeping them in your property. I've not owned property long enough, but I've met landlords who have had the same tenant in a property for 20 or 30 years. Can you imagine? That would be a dream come true.

Now, realistically, it's not likely for tenants to stay that long. Typically, a few years is all you get as life happens to tenants and they need to move. They decide to buy a house, get a new job, get married, get divorced, have children, etc. They will move for all sorts of reasons, but you want to do all you can to make sure they are not moving because they are unhappy about the way you've treated them or the condition of the property.

The problem I see with these houses where the tenants have been renting for 20 or 30 years is that they are almost always rented below market. They were initially rented at the market rate, but the landlords fail to increase rent as the market rises. Obviously, it costs more to rent a house today than it did twenty years ago.

So, I recommend analyzing your properties each year and determining if the market rent has risen. If you have a great tenant, you might not go to the max possible. You don't want to encourage them to leave. But, if market rent is $1,000, and you are only charging $700, you are shortchanging yourself. At $300 per month, that's $3,600 per year. Over ten years, that's $36K!

If you raise the rent $300 per month in one year, that tenant is likely to move. It's too much. So, if you do this, go ahead and plan to find a new tenant in most cases. A better strategy is to gradually raise rents by $50 or so along the way. Don't wait and raise it a large amount all at one time. Some landlords will even have it built into the lease where it will raise by a flat rate of $25 per month every year or 3% to 4% or whatever. This might be a strategy you want to use.

We've done it both ways, and there are pros and cons to each. Some tenants get upset about the automatic increases, and others do not. Our preference is to simply analyze each property every year. The bottom line is make sure you are staying current on the market rent and making small adjustments as the market changes.

On the flip side, remember that turning a unit can sometimes cost a few thousand dollars, so you want to be smart about rent increases. Some owners and landlords prefer to leave the rent where it is as long as the tenant is paying and taking care of the place. This reduces the risk of an unnecessary turn.

PROFESSIONAL PROPERTY MANAGEMENT

If all of this seems daunting or too much to handle, consider hiring a professional property manager. This will allow your investment to be more passive and take a lot of stress off of you. It allows you to focus more on growing your real estate portfolio, growing your business, or whatever else you do, and allows your investment to work without your daily involvement. This is what makes real estate so great. It can be almost completely hands off and produce great returns.

When I first started owning rental properties, I managed them myself. I now own a property management brokerage, Iron Horse Property Management, so I have a property manager as an employee who handles everything with my properties. We also offer our services to other landlords and property owners in the Athens, Georgia area. If you are in our area, I welcome you to contact us. I can say from experience, that it is so worth it to have someone else meet prospective tenants, screen them, sign leases, and handle repairs. My time is better spent doing bigger things to move my businesses forward.

Now, I don't even think about my rentals until there is a big decision to make. Of course, I analyze them annually and make sure repairs and maintenance are happening, and I oversee our property manager, but the property manager is doing the day-to-day activities. I'm not coordinating repairs or looking for a rent check each month for each property. I simply see the direct deposit in my account each month.

Property management fees can vary in different markets but for single family homes, they typically range around the 8% to 10% of the rent per month. Often you'll also see a procurement fee and renewal fee. For a larger property like a large apartment complex the fees may be much lower. But, it's more cost effective to manage 400 properties on one site than it is 400 houses in different locations.

If you decide to hire a property manager, make sure you check references and hire a good one. As with anything else, all property management companies are not equal. My team and I have taken over properties that were managed by other property managers, and we've been able to get them leased faster and for more money than the previous managers. Many of our accounts are taking over properties where owners were self-managing them. Our fee is small enough that usually if we can lease it for $100 per month more, then we cover our fee and the owner makes more money without the headaches.

Even when owners hire professional managers, they often aren't maximizing their ROI if the property manager is not diligent. A great property manager can make you a lot of money, and a bad one can cost you a lot of money. So, don't just look for the one with the lowest fee or the cheapest rate. Look for one that's going to look out for your best interest and manage the property in the best way possible. You want a company that will do all they can to minimize your expenses while maximizing your ROI. You want someone that knows how to do necessary repairs and maintenance cost effectively while saying no to unnecessary repairs. This must be balanced in such a way to keep the tenants happy too, so they will stay year after year. It takes knowledge and expertise to balance this properly.

Many management companies charge a large tenant procurement fee, often equal to one month's rent to procure new tenants. That means if they procure a new tenant each year, they can charge that large fee each year in addition to the monthly fees. This is backwards. Why should you incentivize your property manager to go find new tenants every year? This is costly to you because you pay the fee, but you also pay to turn the unit each time. You are paying for general cleaning, carpet cleaning, painting, etc. At Iron Horse Property Management, we have a compensation structure in place to incentivize our managers to keep tenants rather than re-leasing the units each year. We understand how important it is to work to keep tenants in the properties longer if possible. Our structure creates a win for both our owners and for us as the management company.

Bottom line, investigate the management company you are thinking of hiring and hire the best one. Don't look for the cheapest, and you probably also don't need the most expensive. Even still, know that trying to save 1% or 2% on management fees could end up costing you thousands of dollars in the long run if you hire a bad management company.

Whether you decide to manage the property yourself or hire a professional, just remember, the way it's managed can make the difference between whether the property proves to be a good investment or a bad one. Don't underestimate the value of proper management. If we can help, visit us at www.IronHorseProperty Management.com.

Not only should the property be managed properly, but the tenants should be as well. Let's look at how to manage tenants in the next chapter.

CHAPTER 12
Managing Tenants

When most people think of property management and a property management company, they think of just that . . . managing the property. As in, managing the structure, making repairs, maintaining the lawn, etc.

Most don't think about the fact that managing the tenant is just as important as managing the property. The tenant is the source of the revenue that the property will generate each month. If you have a tenant with a steady job and great credit score, it's going to be easier to make sure that property continues to produce cash every month.

However, if you lease to a tenant who bounces from job to job with periods of unemployment and who has bad credit, that property will not generate consistent income. It might be sporadic from the tenant getting behind and then catching up (or trying to catch up). Over the years, I have learned that once they get behind, they rarely ever catch up. Or even worse, income will be sporadic because they are moving out or being evicted for non-payment, so it's vacant for a while. Then the cycle starts all over again.

Placing a qualified tenant is of utmost importance. We've learned that by using an application process and really vetting tenants on the front end, then most of the time, you can find a very qualified tenant that will pay rent on time every single month.

Once the right tenant is placed, managing the expectations of the tenant is the next big step that many landlords and property managers miss. It's huge when it comes to your relationship with them. If a tenant expects something and doesn't get it, they become upset. And if they stay upset, they are likely to leave at the end of the lease term or sometimes leave early. Be clear upfront on what fixes will or will not be done. And within reason, do what you can to make them happy and to let them know that you care about their well-being while they are living in your property. If there is a safety or habitability issue that needs addressing, make sure you handle it promptly.

If they aren't happy with you or with something about the property and they leave after only one year, it's costly to you. When you lease to a qualified tenant and you treat them properly and manage expectations, they are less likely to leave.

As we discussed earlier, turning a rental unit is when you typically see some of your biggest expenses. My goal on my properties and for owners that we manage properties for is to place tenants, keep them happy, and keep them in the property for as long as possible.

QUALIFICATION CRITERIA

Finding a qualified tenant first starts with screening them. We screen them by taking an online application through our management software. If you are using a professional property manager, they should have an easy way to screen tenants. If not, find a new manager. I can't stress this enough. Finding good tenants can make owning rental property a dream. Placing unqualified tenants can turn that dream into a nightmare!

If you are managing the property yourself, there are several websites where you can sign up and pay a fee to run credit reports, criminal background checks, etc.

When we screen a tenant, we look at credit, income, past rental history, criminal background, and rental references. You can determine your own qualifications for tenants that you lease to, but you want to be consistent. Legally you can't choose someone just because you like them or deny them because you don't like them. You need to have an application process and have certain qualifications.

Credit Score: our current qualifications are that they must have a minimum of 580 credit score, make three times the monthly rent each month, and have good recommendations from past landlords. Often, we get multiple applications and sometimes multiple tenants qualify. In that case, we take the most qualified.

You will need to determine your own criteria for how you will evaluate tenants. You may choose to accept a higher or lower credit score. For most lending institutions to finance a borrower to purchase a home, the minimum score is generally 620. Some lenders are a little higher and some a little lower. You could use 620 as your minimum.

We use 580 because it's high enough to show us that a person consistently pays their bills and it's not too much lower than what would be required to purchase a home. However, it gives us an opportunity to rent to people who fall between 580 and 620. These are people who may otherwise buy a home, and they may be trying to get their score up in order to purchase a home later. If you set your requirement too high, you might miss out on some great tenants that might just have a low score due to some late medical payments or due to a time when they were just having difficulties financially. Often, it's the unexpected medical payments and the like that set applicants back.

Employment: we also want to see a long history of employment, and if they've been on the same job for a while, that's excellent. Of course, sometimes tenants are new to the area and are starting a new job. So, you'll need to consider that. Look for consistent employment. I don't like to see gaps in employment. It makes it difficult for people to pay rent when they are unemployed.

Income Verification: always call the employer to verify that they are employed and in good standing. You also want to ask for a W-2 or check stubs to verify that they do indeed make the amount of money they stated on their application. Make sure to look closely at pay stubs as some people are paid weekly, some bi-monthly, and some monthly. You don't want to look at a monthly paycheck and think it's bi-monthly, or a bi-monthly check and think they get paid that much every week.

Don't ever just take their word for anything. Some people know what you expect on the application and know how to work the system to get what they want. Always verify!

References: lastly, we call their past landlords and property managers, and simply ask if they would lease to the applicant again and if they paid rent on time. Some individuals will just start talking and not stop, so listen. They will tell you the good, the bad, and the ugly.

Don't only call the current landlord or property manager. Make sure to go deeper to the previous ones as well. The current one may tell you what you want to hear because it helps them get rid of a problem tenant. Most owners and property managers won't do this, but some will. It's great to hear from landlords who just can't say enough good things about the tenants. However, if they say they would not lease to them again, even if they don't give you a reason, be very cautious.

FAIR HOUSING LAWS

The reason you want to have criteria for how you select tenants is so that you make sure you don't violate fair housing laws. Fair housing laws protect people in the following classes: race, color, religion, national origin, sex, disability, and familial status. You cannot refuse to lease to someone based on any of those protected classes. You can refuse to rent to them if they have a bad credit score or if they don't make enough money.

Without a set criteria, you can get yourself into trouble if you lead anyone to believe that you discriminated against them based on the protected classes.

For the first five protected classes—race, color, religion, national origin, sex—for most landlords and property managers, it is easy to understand how to be fair and avoid discrimination. You can't refuse to rent to someone simply because they are from a certain country or of a certain religion. You can't refuse them simply because they are male, female, gay, or lesbian. You can't refuse them if they are of a certain race. You must see all people as people and see them equally regardless of any of these characteristics.

Disability sometimes seems to be a little trickier for some people. Reasonable accommodations and modifications must be made for tenants who are disabled. This may include allowing a service animal that helps with the disability even if you have a no pet policy. It also includes allowing the tenant to make modifications to increase accessibility. For example, if the tenant wants to add a wheelchair ramp or modify the shower or the countertop height, they must be allowed to do so. The tenant would make these changes at their own expense, and the law requires that they restore it to its original condition upon move-out. Legally, you can't deny them the opportunity to make changes.

Familial status can also sometimes be one that can get an inexperienced owner in trouble. I've heard old-timer landlords say they don't like to lease to families with children because children, like pets, can cause more damage. Discriminating for this reason is illegal.

So, make sure you don't accept or deny applicants based on any of the protected classes. These protected classes should not even be taken into account. You should only be looking at your criteria of qualifications like income, credit, and references. Remember, you need to be consistent and not change it to make it work for one person and not for another. Always look to lease to the most qualified applicant.

PETS

You can't deny someone from having an animal if the animal aids with their disability. However, you can have a no pet policy that would exclude regular pets.

Most tenants have pets, so if you don't allow pets, you reduce the odds of finding a tenant quickly and you rule out a large percentage of the population. I personally fought this for a long time on some of my nicer properties. I didn't want to allow pets and deal with the damage that might occur. However, after having properties sit vacant for too long, I changed my mind on this policy.

I allow pets now in my personal properties, and I recommend you do also but place some restrictions on it. Set a limit to the number of pets they can have, size restrictions, breed restrictions, etc. Allow the pets, but charge either a one-time pet fee, an additional deposit, or a monthly pet rent. These fees or payments can offset most damage a pet might cause. If you collect an additional month's rent because you leased it earlier by agreeing to take on a pet owner, that can go a long way toward damage as well.

You might choose only to allow small dogs under a certain weight, no more than two animals, etc. As the landlord, you can create these policies and it's not discrimination—again, unless the animal is due to a disability and is a legitimate service animal. Then you must allow it.

You can also state that if an animal is vicious or has ever bitten anyone in the past, that it won't be allowed. Some landlords and even insurance policies limit certain breeds of dogs based on their tendency to attack. Accordingly, you can even limit certain breeds of dogs if you like.

Whatever your policies and rules, be upfront with the tenants. Set the expectations from the beginning of when you expect rent to be paid, who takes care of the lawn, and general rules that you expect to be followed. This information should be in your lease. But, do you think they will read the lease? Many don't, so it's worth talking through it with them as well to make sure they understand. This will save you a lot of headaches in the future.

RENT COLLECTION AND EVICTION

The lease we use states that rent is due on the first and late on the third of each month. I understand that sometimes people forget to pay or whatever, but if it's not paid by the third, we assess a late fee. If they still don't pay, we send a demand notice, and if they still don't pay, we initiate the process of eviction.

Because we do a great job screening our tenants, it's rare that we have evictions, and the vast majority of our rent is in our account by the first of each month. We make it easy for our tenants to pay online with ACH or a credit card, so they really have no excuse not to pay. And because they have good credit and have been screened, we don't have to worry too much. It really pays to have a qualification process and to screen tenants well.

When I bought my first rental properties, I managed them myself. I really didn't have a screening process or any kind of systems to run by. I merely met tenants, and if they were interested and told me they made enough money, I would rent to them. Stupid, I know. And this was years ago. But, I did it.

Then after the first couple of months, I didn't get rent. When I would contact them, they would have some excuse about work, family, or some unforeseen event. I've heard excuse after excuse after excuse. Some of them were probably true, and some probably not true. Either way, I was getting excuses rather than the rent money I should have been getting.

Also, as a novice landlord, I would feel compassion for them and give them more time to pay. It was this process that taught me that tenants rarely catch up once they are behind. I also learned the process of evicting tenants this way. I was left with no choice once they became 3 to 4 months behind on rent. For some property owners, this process alone makes it worth professional management. Owning rental real estate must be treated like a business, and if you can't do that, you should hire someone who will.

I should have never waited that long, and experienced landlords would laugh at me for waiting that long. The reality is that these tenants knew how to work me and how to take advantage of me. I would give them an inch, and they would take a mile. And it happened to me more than once. So, if you are a new landlord, don't fall into the same trap I did when I first started. Learn from my mistakes!

I learned a lot since the early days of owning rental property. Had I screened properly and leased to qualified tenants, as we do now, I would not have gone through it. However, I learned from it. I learned what to do when I do need to evict, but more than that, I learned how not to have to evict (most of the time). I learned how to properly screen tenants so that it rarely becomes necessary. If you manage enough properties, eventually you'll encounter evictions or an early move-out, but doing the work on the front end will almost eliminate the need for evictions.

SECURITY DEPOSIT & MOVE-IN INSPECTION

Upon leasing the unit, you also need to collect a security deposit in addition to the first month's rent. Believe it or not, sometimes tenants will ask you if they can pay the security deposit in installments over 2 to 3 months. Do not allow this! Honestly, if a tenant is asking that question, they likely are not qualified, but even if they are, get the security deposit upfront. This is a game the tenants will play, and you will likely not get your deposit and find yourself short on timely rent payments as well. If they don't have their deposit, then they probably aren't managing their money very well.

In Georgia, the security deposit cannot be collected until the initial move-in inspection has been completed. You'll need to complete a walk-through or move-in inspection where the tenant has the right to point out any flaws, such as stains on the carpet, a chip in the countertop, or any damages that might be in the house prior to their move-in. The purpose of this inspection is simply to note flaws that are already present, so the tenant doesn't get penalized with a deduction from the security deposit at the end of the lease. If a problem is pre-existing, then it's not the tenant's fault, so deductions cannot and should not be taken. Flaws are documented for each room of the house and signed by you and the tenant. If the items are listed on their move-in inspection, then you cannot deduct for that upon move-out. And without a move-in inspection, you legally can't keep any of their security deposit if there are damages upon move-out.

At my property management company, we've actually taken over management on properties from individuals who had previously managed themselves and had failed to conduct move-in inspections.

Upon move-out, we have to explain that we legally must return the security deposit in full even if there are damages. So, make sure you complete a move-in inspection and get it signed prior to accepting the security deposit and prior to move-in. It's small mistakes like these that owners sometimes make when managing property on their own. They either lose money because something wasn't done right, or they find themselves in legal trouble if the tenant disputes something.

Also, make sure you set the expectation that the move-in inspection is not intended to be a punch-out list of items that you will come back and repair. Upon signing the lease, they agree to accept the property "as is," and the purpose of the move-in inspection is to note flaws, so they aren't charged for them later. That means you are not going to replace carpet because there is a stain in the bedroom or repair the chipped countertop or replace the missing piece of trim behind the bathroom door. None of these things affect the habitability of the house or tenant safety. But having it on the move-in list does prevent the tenant from being charged for it later.

REPAIRS

If you set the expectation early that you will repair any little thing the tenant asks for, you might be doing repairs non-stop. Some will call you and complain that the dishwasher is too loud and tell you that they want a newer model. They will call and say that the floor creaks in one spot, and they want it replaced or that the icemaker doesn't make ice fast enough. You should not be catering to tenants' every little complaint. If you set the expectation upfront, they'll know not to even ask. However, if you don't set the expectation, they'll have you out there every week doing something!

Now, obviously, if something is broken, you need to repair it in a timely manner. And if something is broken, you want to know about it. We classify repairs as "low priority," "priority," or "emergency."

Low-priority repairs are things like doors not closing properly or a ceiling fan not operating. These are repairs that need to be addressed, but they are not urgent. We try to handle these kinds of maintenance requests within a few days.

Priority repairs are things like a toilet continuously running, a dripping faucet, a failing appliance, or an air conditioning unit that's not cooling. We like to get on these repairs within a day if possible.

Emergency repairs are things that involve water going where it should not be going, burning smells, gas smells, etc. These are the kinds of repairs that may jeopardize tenant safety or that could potentially cause major damage to the house. Water can quickly cause lots of problems and we want to address any leaks or flooding immediately. If there is a gas leak or electrical issue that could cause a fire or endanger the tenant, we want to address those immediately as well.

At my management company, we have a special phone number that goes to three team members at the same time for emergencies to make sure we respond in a timely manner even after hours or on the weekends. If you are managing your property on your own, you want to make sure you are accessible to address emergencies as they may arise.

You want to provide the tenant with a nice, safe, comfortable home, and you need to remember that you want them to stay for many years. So, it's a balancing act of keeping them happy while also not letting them run you crazy over every little repair. It all comes down to setting expectations upfront and keeping the house maintained and in good shape.

Now that you know the benefits of owning rental property and how to manage the property and the tenants, you must decide how much you will do on your own and how much you will rely on trusted advisors. Surrounding yourself with experts can help you to build your portfolio faster and with fewer mistakes to save you time and money. Let's look into it more in the next chapter.

CHAPTER 13
Upping the Pace with Your Dream Team

Most would agree that individuals all have different strengths and weaknesses. Some people are very detail-oriented whereas others are more big-picture-oriented. I've learned that in life, I can go much further and must faster in my investment and entrepreneurial pursuits with the help of other people. The lone wolf in business or investing rarely goes very far.

If your goal is to grow a rental portfolio that will take care of you and your family in the future, you are going to need the support of others. You are going to need a team. As I've stated earlier in this book, I believe a true partnership where equity and duties are split between partners should be entered into very cautiously. It is terrific when the right people are paired together but can ruin friendships and businesses when things go awry.

YOUR DREAM TEAM

The definition of "team" in the context of this chapter is not a team of your employees and not true equity partners. What I'm referring to is a team of individuals who are key players and experts in helping you move your investing forward at a faster pace. These people will help you find deals, help you to save money in the process, and can prevent you from making big mistakes. They can see things that you won't always see. These will be your advisors for various aspects of your investing business.

Who am I referring to? I'm referring to a lender, real estate agent, home inspector, insurance agent, property manager, handyman, building contractor, landscaper, and others. If you don't have these key players in place, then you are these people. As you've gathered from my early experiences like letting late rent payments slide and such, I've learned firsthand that rather than trying to be a "jack of all trades (and master of none)," it's better to have key people in place who are experts in their chosen field. You want to have these relationships built and strong before and during your investing career.

These are people that you may call partners, team members, or simply business associates. The bottom line is that you need to like these people and you need to have a good working relationship with them. Your relationship will be mutually beneficial for you and them in that they will help you in advancing your investing business, but you are also helping them make income by using their services. Let's consider each team member in a little more detail.

YOUR MONEY PEOPLE

Obviously, you must have a lender or banker in place that's ready to fund the deals that you are going to buy, unless, of course, you have the cash. If you have enough cash or a partner with cash, then you can fund your own deals and you won't need a lender. If you don't have the cash or if you simply want to use leverage, then you'll need to have an individual in place that you can call and quickly get a preapproval letter from or an idea of the terms and payment on a deal you are considering.

If you are buying a move-in ready home, this may be a traditional mortgage lender. This is where you simply put down 20% of the purchase price, close, and rent the house. As detailed in chapter 7, with a traditional mortgage lender, you can get a fixed-rate mortgage for 30 or 15 years. You need a trusted individual mortgage lender or mortgage lending team that can be your go-to whenever you are acquiring a new property. You may need a preapproval letter, or you may have questions about the terms of a deal at a certain price. By having a relationship with this person or team, you can quickly get answers and get what you need. This individual would also typically have most of your financial information on file, so you can get quick answers and move fast.

If you are buying a house that will require work, you are more likely to need a local banker. Also, as mentioned in chapter 7, if you are holding title to properties in a corporation or LLC, then you'll need a local bank. The local banks can typically close faster than a traditional mortgage lender, and their closing fees are typically less. Also, they can more easily devise loans that will give you funding to repair homes as well if you are purchasing a fixer-upper. A local bank loan usually just works better for those types of deals.

You are going to need both a mortgage lender and a local banker on your team. If you start out working with a private lender or hard money lender, that's fine, but you'll need to transition to a lender with lower rates. I recommend you have a more traditional lender to refinance you out of those high interest hard money loans. If you stay with those types of loans, you'll spend way too much in interest and likely fail with investing.

YOUR REAL ESTATE EXPERT

If you are new to investing in real estate, I highly recommend you find an expert real estate agent in your market to assist you. Even if you are a more seasoned investor, a good agent can prove to be very valuable as they can give you insight on certain parts of town and values in certain areas.

Having a real estate agent that's knowledgeable about investing and able to commit to helping you find great deals is essential to your success. As an investor, if you are out beating the bushes and searching online, you are sure to find some good buys on your own. However, being a real estate broker myself, I know firsthand, that as agents, we often hear of and know of deals before the public knows about them, as exemplified in my stories from chapter 6. These are often the best deals and are sold before they ever make it online to the multiple listing services or to websites like Zillow.

In order to have an advantage and get the best deals, you are going to need a real estate agent on your team that's working for you and tipping you off to some of these deals. Sometimes it's a seller they meet with directly, and other times it may be through networking with other agents, but a top real estate agent or agent team will be beneficial to your success. Agents can also help you to write up offers and negotiate through pricing and repairs.

I want to give you a word of caution about selecting your agent. It's been proven in the industry that the top 20% of agents sell 80% of the real estate. I encourage you to find an agent or team that's in the top 20% and also work with an agent that has investment property themselves so that they have a better understanding of your goals and what makes a great rental property. They can give you insight that an average agent may not be able to give.

You may have concerns that the agent will buy all of the best deals themselves before you can. I don't think this is a valid concern. Even if the agent is an investor, they can't buy all the deals, and most are honest enough that they will not buy something out from under their client. If they do, find a new agent. But again, I don't think this should give you cause for concern. Their expertise through owning their own property and being an investor themselves will serve you much better than working with an agent that doesn't understand investment real estate.

The other problem when selecting a real estate agent to partner with is that it's relatively easy to get a real estate license in most states. I've been in this business for years, and I've seen thousands of agents come into the business and exit the business in less than a year. In most states, it takes more education to get a cosmetology license than it does a real estate license. I'm sharing this information with you because it's easy to get connected with a novice agent or even an agent with many years of experience but very little expertise.

Be sure to interview and hire an agent that is an expert in your market and also one that understands investment property. On the flip side, there are some top agents who feel they don't have time to work with investors because they would rather spend their time working with luxury buyers and selling higher priced homes.

Finding the right agent to partner with is key to your success, so don't just pick this at random. Find the one that's going to serve you and look for one that you can have a long-lasting relationship with for years to come as you purchase more and more properties.

We are building a network of investment agents throughout the country that are experienced with investing in real estate. These agents own rental property themselves and have experience with it. Some of these agents have even been through our investment agent training course, so they understand how to help you analyze investment property and how to calculate your returns. If you would like some assistance in finding the right agent in your area to help you find rental properties, visit our website at www.TheRealEstateWayBook.com/findagent.

YOUR HOME INSPECTOR

Once you start locating some homes that you are interested in buying and once you start writing offers and getting homes under contract, you are going to need to get the home inspected during your due diligence period to make sure there are no hidden surprises. At my firm, we typically recommend that all of our buyers negotiate a due diligence period (or inspection period) to allow time to inspect the property, investigate the neighborhood, etc., and make 100% sure they want to move forward with the deal. When you negotiate a due diligence period into your contract, you have an opportunity to back out or renegotiate if problems are found during that time period. Contracts are different from state to state, so I recommend you ask your agent about a due diligence or inspection period when writing your offer. At my firm, we don't recommend a contract without a due diligence period unless it's a unique situation or it's one of our seasoned and sophisticated investor clients and they insist on offering without it.

If you don't hire a home inspector, then it's up to you to inspect it yourself. However, all of my agents and I highly recommend you get a professional home inspection. Just like real estate agents, some of these home inspectors are great and others not as great. The good ones inspect two or three houses every day, so they know what to look for and how to find problems and potential problems. They have a trained eye that you likely do not have.

I would advise you to lean on your real estate agent for recommendations for a home inspector so that you find a great one. The purpose of a home inspection is so that you have a clear understanding of exactly what you are buying. As you listen to the inspector and review the report, you'll know what's great about the house, any problems, and potential future problems. When the home is inspected, you want to focus on the expensive items that need attention or repairs, and the major systems that may be in their last days and may need replacement soon. All homes are going to need some odd-and-end repairs. Don't get caught up in the small items that are easily repaired. There are no perfect houses, so don't have the wrong expectation going in. If you are waiting to find and buy a perfect house, you'll never buy one.

Regardless of what's needed, use this inspection report as you analyze your property and get an estimate of what your total investment will be and any major expenses that might come up in the near future. If the furnace is near the end of its useful life, you'll need to anticipate possibly replacing it in the next few years. And that's OK as long as you are getting a good deal on the house. Sometimes your agent can even negotiate for the seller to make a few of these repairs or to adjust the price to compensate for the repairs.

YOUR INSURANCE AGENT

Prior to closing on the home, you are going to need to have insurance in place. I recommend having one agency that you can call for all of your real estate needs. This can likely be the same company that has your current home and auto. I prefer working with local agents as opposed to the online companies, but the important thing is that you have insurance in place. If you are getting a loan on the property, the lender will force you to do this. If not, you especially need insurance. It would be a bad day if you paid cash for a house, didn't get insurance, and it burned down.

By having one agent that knows your objectives and understands your goals, they can advise you on what kind of insurance you need. It may be that in addition to insurance on the home, you may need to add an umbrella policy or some additional coverage as you grow your portfolio. Find an agent that understands your needs and can make recommendations.

Also, by having an insurance agent that handles all of your properties and knows your needs, you can get a policy in place quickly and efficiently. They will already know what kind of coverage you need, your preferred deductible, etc.

I was closing on a purchase once that didn't involve bank financing, and at the closing table I realized that I had not yet put insurance in place. Because I was paying cash, I didn't have the lender to remind me and confirm that I had insurance. So, that house was going to be mine in less than an hour and it had no insurance. I was able to call my agent from the closing attorney's office and get insurance in place immediately. Without a prior relationship, it would not have happened that fast. This particular house was tenant-occupied, so if I didn't have insurance in place and they burned it down later that day or if a big storm came through, I could have potentially lost tens of thousands of dollars. Having a trusted relationship with a great insurance agent is vital for your success.

YOUR PROPERTY MANAGER

You've already learned in a previous chapter the importance of property management to the success of your rental property. Unless you are confident in your own ability to screen and place tenants, conduct move-in inspections, collect rent, uphold the terms of the lease, evict when necessary, handle repairs, etc., then you need a great property manager.

For a nominal fee, a great property manager will protect your investment and assure your highest return. And, it makes owning rental property a breeze for you. It's one less headache to deal with. For years, I thought I was saving money by managing my rental property myself. It took a few years for me to figure out that my time is better spent building my business and letting someone else handle my rental property. And because I was doing it myself, I was not as efficient or productive as professional management. I made mistakes, like taking too long to lease a property, because I was too busy to show it, and in haste, I leased to some less-than-qualified tenants, which is a disaster.

A professional is worth their weight in gold if they prevent you from leasing to a bad tenant. If they lease it one month faster than you can or for $100 more per month than you can, it's almost like they work for you for free. If you are currently managing property on your own, consider hiring a professional. Once I turned it over to a professional, a lot of stress was removed and I've been able to grow my portfolio even faster.

I would recommend you lean on your local trusted real estate agent or other vendors for a recommendation for a property manager. Sometimes a real estate agent will also do property management, so this person could be one in the same. However, if it's a one-person show, make sure they are capable of both helping you find property and managing your property. They should be great at both. Sales and property management are two very different skill sets, so in most cases, this will be two different individuals. However, sometimes you might find an agent that does great at both.

Your Repair Crew

You'll also need a good handyman and/or building contractor as you start acquiring properties. The handyman will be your first call for minor repairs and issues as they arise. If you are buying properties in need of extensive repair, you'll need a general building contractor to call on. You can likely contract all of this out to individuals yourself, but for large renovation projects, I've found that a general contractor can handle it all and the outcome is much better.

Once you have the property in service and it's leased, in some instances you may need a more specialized person to help. These would include an HVAC contractor, landscaper, painter, flooring contractor, electrician, and plumber. For example, if the furnace goes out, the handyman probably can't fix that. You don't need to call a general contractor for that either. Call the HVAC company or technician directly. If the property needs to be painted after a tenant moves out, call your trusted painter. They can likely do a better job for a similar price or for less than what the handyman would charge. For many small odd-and-end repairs, like changing a light, repairing a leaky faucet, rotten wood, etc., the handyman will be your first call, as they typically can do lots of things and will be cheaper than a specialist.

If you are using a professional property manager, they will have these contacts and can coordinate these repairs for you once the tenant is in place and the property is under their management. You won't need these contacts if you have a property manager. As previously stated, a good property manager will simplify your life by handling all of the tedious tasks of property management while you enjoy the benefits of ownership.

When you gather a team of professionals around you that are experts in their chosen field, you will reach your investing goals much faster. They are going to help you to make more money and also save you money by minimizing your mistakes. Nothing is completely predictable when it comes to real estate and rental property, but having the right professionals by your side will tremendously increase your odds of success, so don't overlook the importance of surrounding yourself with a team of experts.

Now that you've bought your first property, you have your lease in place, you have a plan, you have a team of experts, and you are making some passive cash flow, how do you buy the next one? And the one after that? This is called scaling, and it's the subject of the next chapter.

CHAPTER 14
Scaling to Multiple Properties

Acquiring more and more properties, and scaling your real estate investments takes focused effort. However, once you buy your first one and get started, buying more becomes easier. You become more confident since you've done it before, and your success will make you want more success.

As time goes on, your debt will decrease on your properties, and most likely they will appreciate in value. This gives you a lot of leverage to continue buying. As you buy more properties, the debt also gets reduced on those, they appreciate in value, and your net worth will grow, allowing you the resources and leverage to buy even more properties. It will begin to snowball.

SMART AND NOT-SO-SMART

As I've already done, again I caution you against overleveraging. This is when you borrow too much and you are unable to service the debt from the rent you are collecting. Keep plenty of margin here so that even with some vacancies, you can service the debt.

The economic downturn in 2008 to 2012 was the demise of many investors. The ones that were overleveraged lost everything to the banks. The ones who were not overleveraged continued to pay down their debt with rental income and came out of that recession unscathed.

The really smart investors were well capitalized during the Great Recession, meaning they had money in the bank or access to funding other than traditional banks. In turn, they were able to double or triple their portfolios. Some did even better, made millions, and their net worth soared coming out of that downturn. Even in my local market, homes that I would consider perfect rentals were selling for 50 cents on the dollar compared to pre-recession, and now in 2018, they are worth even more than they were before the collapse!

For example, in my area, homes that were selling for around $130K to $140K during 2006 and 2007 could be easily purchased in 2011 and 2012 for around $70K. They were abundant and not hard to find. They were listed on multiple listing services, and you had plenty to choose from. You could shop and pick the best one, and they were all priced from $70K to $90K even in good condition.

Today, in 2018, these same homes are selling around $160K to $180K. My regret is not buying as many of those homes as possible at the bottom of the market. Hindsight is always 20/20, right? I wish I had partnered with someone that had cash during those times. I personally did not have the funds to invest on my own then.

Fewer homes were selling during those days, so my commission income as an agent was greatly reduced. My wife and I were actually dipping into our savings just to pay our personal bills. But, guess what? We kept all of our rental properties that we had acquired previously. We came out of it owing less than we did going in. Tenants made those payments for us. We just had the benefit of owning the homes. We couldn't sell them to generate cash because those homes were only worth about what we owed on them. We were forced to keep them and are thankful we did.

Just imagine if we had owned more homes or if we had owned them free and clear at that time? That revenue would have protected our savings account, and it also would have possibly allowed us to purchase some of those deals that were so abundant at that time.

I expect you can see why I'm so passionate about owning rental property!

OPTIONS FOR BIG GROWTH

There are a few options for growing your portfolio, so let's consider them.

We've already discussed in chapter 8 the "moving method," where you buy a house for a personal residence, live in it a few years, then purchase another primary residence. Rather than selling, you keep the previous residence as a rental property. This can be a great strategy, but to really scale faster, you need more strategies.

STRATEGY 1: THE TRADE-IN

In this strategy, you sell a property as the value rises and debt decreases, take that equity and use it to make down payments to buy two more. You are basically trading in one property in exchange for two. Then in a few years, sell those two, and use that equity to buy four. Then continue to use this strategy to exponentially grow your portfolio.

To see how that strategy could play out let's look at the example below. Notice the example uses estimated numbers, and I have not included real estate commissions or other selling expenses. This example is for illustrative purposes only to show you how to think.

Year 1   You buy one house for $125,000 with a mortgage of $100,000, and it appreciates at an average of 4% per year.

Year 5   It's now worth $150,000, and you owe $90,000 due to the debt reduction. That's a spread of $60,000 when you sell. Using a 1031 tax-deferred exchange (see chapter 10), you take the $60,000 and buy two more houses, putting $30,000 down on each one.

Year 10   You sell those two (similarly to how you sold the one house in year 5) and buy four homes.

Year 15   You sell those four (similarly to how you sold the two houses in year 10) and buy eight.

You get the picture. This example uses only the initial investment of $25K in year one. So if you continue to save and invest additional income from your job each year, this strategy will compound and scale much faster.

You can continue using this trade-in strategy in future years to multiply your portfolio. Again, it's never going to work out perfectly, and some homes will appreciate more than others and some less. I'm working from an average.

Notice in the example, I incorporated the 1031 tax-deferred exchange as a part of the strategy. Without using it, you would be subject to capital gains taxes. Revisit chapter 10 if you need a reminder of the significance of the 1031 tax-deferred exchange and capital gains taxes.

If your properties are good performers, sometimes it's better not to sell them, but to simply refinance them, pull out that equity, and use the cash from the refinance to buy another property. When you do this, make sure the rent will cover your new debt service and still produce cash flow.

STRATEGY 2: CASH-OUT REFINANCE

Theoretically, as long as you have positive cash flow of even a dollar after all expenses and debt service, you can grow and continue adding properties. Just remember, the more you leverage, the more risk you have. An unexpected change in the market or change in the economy impacts you in a bigger way if you are overleveraged. I like to cash flow at least $200 to $300 per property after expenses and debt service. This works out to around 20% to 30% of the rent. If your cash flow is too low, it can be tough to survive if the rental market does soften a bit. For example, if your cash flow is only $50 per month and the market rent decreases by $100 per month, you suddenly go from making $50 each month to losing $50 each month. If this happens over multiple properties, it can be hard to overcome.

See below the example of how a cash-out refinance could enable you to acquire more properties.

Year 1   You buy one house for $125,000 with a mortgage of $100,000, and it appreciates at an average of 4% per year.

Year 5   It's now worth $150,000 and you owe $90,000. You refinance. The lender will give you up to 80% of the appraised value. So, you are able to pull out $30,000. You can use this $30,000 to put a down payment on another home. Now you own two rentals.

Year 10   You refinance both of these homes again, and buy two more homes for a total of four homes.

Then, you continue this process. This is a slow process, but it does not include you adding any of your own funds to your portfolio. This cash-out strategy uses the first house you purchase to fund the purchases of additional homes in the future.

STRATEGY 3: THE SAVER'S WAY

If you are able to save enough money each year to invest in a down payment to buy one house every year, you can then use these same strategies to grow your portfolio much faster. About every five years, you can refinance or sell in order to purchase more. Using the same information in the examples above, but by investing around $25K per year into real estate rather than your retirement fund, it can grow more rapidly. See below.

Year 1   You invest $25,000 for a down payment to buy one home.

Year 2   You invest $25,000 for a down payment to buy another home. You now own two.

Year 3   You invest $25,000 for a down payment to buy another home for a total of three.

Year 4   You invest $25,000 for a down payment to buy another home for a total of four.

Year 5   You invest $25,000 for a down payment to buy another home and refinance the home bought in year 1 to buy a second property that year for a total of six homes.

Year 6   You invest $25,000 for a down payment to buy another home and refinance the property bought in year 2 to buy another home for a total of eight homes.

Year 7   You invest $25,000 for a down payment to buy another home and refinance the property bought in year 3 to buy another home for a total of ten homes.

Then you'd continue working to invest more and using the equity and cash flow from existing properties to continue building your portfolio. It can grow exponentially this way.

If you are not financially able to save a down payment every year, then do it every other year or as often as possible. If you are not able to save $25K per year for a down payment, but you can save $10,000, then you can use the above scenario and run it every 2.5 years instead of every year. Then it would take about twenty years instead of seven years.

The speed you go is dependent upon the funds you have to invest, the deals you are able to find, and the general market conditions. Eventually the cash flow from the properties will give you your down payment each year. When you build up to ten houses, cash flowing $300 per month, that's $36K per year . . . That's enough for a down payment on another house each year just from the cash produced from your rental homes!

At some point, when you build up to ten or twenty homes, you might decide to sell half to pay off the other half. If you decide that you can live off of the income of five properties, then try to get your portfolio to ten homes, then sell off five to pay off or mostly pay off the other five. Once even a portion of those are paid off, your monthly income will rise significantly, allowing you the means to pay off the other homes even faster.

Strategy 4: The All-Cash Approach

Another option to grow your portfolio is to simply start out paying cash and let the cash flow build and snowball. This is a more conservative approach and takes longer, but it works. You really almost need to buy your first property with cash in order to get enough traction for this approach to work. Otherwise, it simply takes too long.

Here's an example of how that might look. As you can see, this approach will also snowball in time, and the snowball will get bigger and bigger as time goes on.

Year 1   You buy a house for cash for $125,000 that rents for $1,400 per month. After paying taxes, insurance, and repairs, it should net around $12,000 per year.

Year 10   If you save $12,000 per year and add nothing to it, in 10 years, you would have $120,000. In year 10, you buy a second house.

Year 15   After buying the second property, you now have approximately $24,000 coming in each year, so you could buy another house in year 15 for $120,000.

Of course, by investing and saving more from your job, you can speed up this process. Even still, this is a very slow and conservative way to do it.

With any of these strategies, I recommend you continue using as much savings as possible from your job to invest. This requires cutting your expenses down, living on one income, or living on much less than what you make. It requires a lot of sacrifice in the beginning, but after doing this for a few years, you can be free from your job and continue your lifestyle.

As you can see from the above scenarios, the faster you can acquire rental properties, the faster the rent comes in, and the more you can save to reinvest. If you are intentional about this for a few years, you can build quite a portfolio, and then it will begin to build itself. Once you have enough income from the properties to pay all of your bills, you can choose how you spend your time and what you do! Freedom!

Most likely, you'll end up using a combination of these strategies. That's how you get the compound effect in place and can grow really fast. Using one of these strategies alone can cause you to grow, but you'll grow faster by using a combination. Bottom line, the more you are able to invest each year into buying more houses, the faster your portfolio will grow and the faster your cash flow will grow!

No two investors will do things exactly the same way and have the exact same journey. I'm giving you ideas and strategies. Now it's up to you to decide your path. Again, when it gets tough, keep the end goal in mind, and remember why you are doing what you are doing.

YEARLY ANALYSIS

No matter what strategy or combination of strategies you use, I recommend you analyze your properties each year. To do this, you look at the value of the property and decide whether or not you would make that purchase again. Does the property still make sense?

If the value of the property rises at a much faster pace than the rental income (see chapter 5), it might be time to sell it and put that equity to work for a higher return. What I mean by that is once home values in a particular neighborhood have gone up so much that the rents have leveled off and won't go higher, you might consider selling.

For example, let's say you purchased a home several years ago for $100K that leased for $1,000 per month. Over time, both the value of the home and the rents increased. So, now it rents for $1,500 per month, and you feel that's the max rent for the area. That's a great return on your initial investment. But, let's say that homes in that neighborhood have appreciated greatly due to the location, and that home is now worth $250K. Would you buy that home today for $250K in order to rent it for $1,500? Probably not. That ROI would not be great. So, you must question whether or not you should keep it. Can you rent it for more? Or have the rents topped out for the area? If you can sell that house and replace it with two more homes that you can purchase for $125K each that would each rent for $1,200 per month, that might be a wise thing to do. You take one property that's generating $1,500 per month in gross income and convert it to $2,400 gross income per month. Your gross income goes from $18,000 per year to $28,800, which is almost $11,000 more per year! That could be a wise thing to do. You'll need to do your homework and know your local market to determine whether this is possible. And then of course, you'll need to evaluate the properties that you purchase to make sure you truly get the return you are looking for.

Remember, when considering whether to sell, consider the tax consequences and make sure it's the right thing to do. I've sold properties in the past and regretted it. The main thing is to make sure that if you sell, you have other homes you can buy to replace this one with greater monthly cash flow for the same investment and equity.

The best time to sell is when a tenant moves out, so you'll have to decide to either not renew a lease or just wait until they voluntarily decide to move.

By analyzing the values of each property annually, I can determine whether to continue holding a property or sell it to replace it with better performers. As your properties appreciate in value, in some instances, you may be able to sell one and take the equity to buy two more.

Depending on your market, you may or may not be able to buy homes for $125K that would rent for $1,200 per month. In my market of Athens, Georgia, this was not difficult just a couple of years ago; however, as values continue to rise, it's getting harder to find these ratios. Currently, at the time of this writing, a house that would rent for $1,200 per month may cost $140K to $150K. However, in time, I expect these rents to rise as well. Even these numbers could give a return of around 7%. And as long as values continue to rise, this strategy of using equity to buy more will continue to work.

I'm constantly looking for better performers. If you continually focus on growing your ROI and increasing the returns on your investments, you'll continue to grow your portfolio, your wealth, and your monthly cash flow. The key is to make the right choices and decisions so that you can maximize your ROI without getting overleveraged.

Once you are producing cash flow, continue to reinvest that cash flow into more properties to create the snowball effect.

Now that you have begun acquiring properties, you must get it leased and you need a written lease that outlines the terms of who will do what and when and how much the rent will be. There are a few different ways you can structure your leases that we'll review in the upcoming chapter.

CHAPTER 15

Leasing Structures for Maximum Returns

How do you structure your leases, outlining the terms of who will do what and when and how much the rent will be? Actually, you have a few options. We'll review the following in this chapter:

- Straight Lease

    o   Completely Custom Lease

    o   Semi-Custom Lease

- Leasing to Students

- Short-Term and Vacation-Rental Leasing

- Lease/Purchase and Lease/Option

- Owner Financing

STRAIGHT LEASE

The most common leasing structure is what I call a straight lease. This is what is done probably 95% of the time in residential leasing. It's the method that I prefer and is most applicable for investing in properties that you intend to hold for the long term, which is what this book is all about.

A straight lease is probably what you are most familiar with as well. You sign a lease with the tenant to pay a certain amount of money each month for a certain term. It could be 12 months, 24 months, or more. This lease will outline when rent is due and any late fees. It will outline all of the details like who is responsible for utilities and who is responsible for lawn maintenance and more.

You'll need to think through these things when you prepare your lease, and you need to have it structured to your desires. In commercial leasing, because it's business-to-business, you'll often see customized lease agreements between the landlord and tenant. Many times, with commercial real estate, attorneys will even negotiate the terms and rack up thousands in fees in the process.

However, on a residential lease, as the owner, you get to call the shots. I've never seen a tenant try to change terms of a residential lease to any degree and succeed. Either they sign the lease, or they don't lease the property. It's usually that simple.

So, make sure to think about all of the elements that you want in the lease and tailor a lease to fit your needs. How do you obtain such a lease?

If you are working with a property manager, they'll have their lease that's legal for your state, so you won't need one. Theirs will have all of the protections you need along with the terms clearly defined. However, if you are going to self-manage, you'll need to have a lease ready.

Many people will simply go online or go to an office supply store and purchase a generic lease. This can work fine, but different states have different laws and what's allowed in one state may not be allowed in another. And, because these leases are generic, they probably don't have the same protections as a customized lease might have. When you are first starting out, this approach may be fine. However, as you grow, you need to think differently. The small things will make a bigger impact over several properties. If you can do something that saves you $200 on one property, it's not a huge deal, but if you can save or make $200 over 25 properties, that's $5,000! Some small things that add up are fees like pet fees, late fees, or cleaning fees. Some landlords will waive the late fee, and some will not charge a cleaning fee back to the tenants after they leave the property a mess when moving out. Allowing these small things to slide will escalate into a lot of money as you own more properties.

As your portfolio gets bigger, the little things will make a bigger difference in your profitability.

COMPLETELY CUSTOM LEASE

To be completely custom you might hire an attorney to draft a lease for you that includes the terms and elements that are important to you. This will come at a cost. However, the same principle applies. If a custom lease costs you $1,000, but you can fill in blanks and use it across all of your properties year after year after year, it's not that big of a deal. If you have 10 homes, that's $100 per home rather than $1,000 for one home.

SEMI-CUSTOM LEASE

A third option would be to get a semi-custom lease, and this is probably the best way to go, especially as you get started and have just a few properties. When I first started out, I bought a lease from a real estate guru in Atlanta. This was a guy who owned several single-family homes that he rented out, and he also taught courses about real estate. He had a lease that an attorney drafted for him, and he had the rights to license out the use of his lease. I purchased it from him for around $100, I think.

That certainly cost a lot more than a lease from an office supply store, but not as much as a custom lease from an attorney. And since he was also in Georgia, as I am, I knew the lease would apply to the homes I was leasing out as well.

I used this lease for years until opening my property management brokerage. Then we got a lease specific for that business that we could use on behalf of our clients.

LEASING TO STUDENTS

If you are planning to be in the student rental business, you'll most likely want a lease with a structure that you can easily add an exhibit or insert language to include parental guarantees. As previously discussed, leasing to college students can be a great strategy, but when a college student has no income, it's hard to qualify them and hard to enforce rent payments. With a parental guarantee, you have much more security.

You will also need a lease tailored in such a way that you can rent to individual students on a "per bedroom" basis. This will likely require a customized lease as most leases are not structured this way. However, many students prefer to sign individual leases per bedroom with common areas being shared between roommates.

The straight lease is most likely what you'll be using in your real estate business, but in some instances, you might need another structure. Some of these structures may include lease option, lease purchase, owner financing, or short-term and vacation-rental leasing. Let's look into those.

SHORT-TERM AND VACATION-RENTAL LEASING

With the growth of websites like VRBO and Airbnb, a whole new market has been created for investors to take advantage of the short-term rental market and compete with hotels. Nightly rentals are the most expensive rental out there, so it can work nicely for investors. It is much more management-intensive, but the returns can be super high, so you must weigh the pros and cons.

Think about the last time you stayed at a hotel. What did you pay? Depending on the quality, it could have been $90 to $400 or more. Multiply that figure by 30 days to get a monthly rate. Do you see what I mean about the high returns for nightly rentals?

Let's imagine for a moment you owned that hotel room and were going to lease it out for a year. How much would it bring in per month? Certainly not $2,700 ($90 * 30) to $12,000 ($400 * 30). No one would pay that much per month for an annual lease. Yes, the returns on short-term rentals can be astronomical. Now clearly, hotel rooms are not always booked 30 out of 30 days. Your vacancy rate will be higher, but with the nightly rental, the returns can be much higher if you can keep it relatively full.

The key to the short-term rental market is to own it in a location that someone will want to vacation or spend a week or a weekend. For example, I live and operate my business in a university town. And being in the South, football is huge. Every hotel room in Athens will be booked during UGA home football games. They will also be completely booked during big events like graduations.

This creates opportunities for investors who own condos close to campus, especially those within a few blocks of the stadium and campus. These investors have two options. They can lease these units on an annual basis to students and get a consistent monthly payment that's relatively hands-off and requires a small amount of their time each month. Or almost none of their time each month if they have a property management company handling things for them.

However, their second option is to lease it through a site like Airbnb. This would allow them to take a two-bedroom condo that might rent for $900 to $1,000 per month and lease it for $200 to $300 per night. As long as they can rent it for four or five nights per month, they will make more money than they would if it were a long-term rental. Everything else is a bonus.

If the condo is in a desirable area, that should be relatively easy to do. My example about football does pose a problem. Football is seasonal, so you'll want to make sure you can lease it other times of the year as well. And most of the investors I know with short-term rentals do. Sometimes, they offer them as weekly rentals for someone who is between housing for 2 to 3 weeks or even for business travelers who may be in town for a project for a short period of just a few weeks.

A rental like this strikes a nice balance between a hotel room and leasing something for a longer period of time. It fills a niche so to speak. For someone who is only going to be in town for a couple of weeks, staying in a condo with a kitchen is much nicer than a hotel. If the rates are similar, it's a win.

Can you see how renting that two-bedroom condo for $150 to $200 per night for a week could be a win for you and a client? A hotel would likely charge that amount as well, but the condo provides more comfort for the traveler.

Of course, vacation rentals are also a short-term rental play. Since I'm not on the beach or in the mountains, I'm not as familiar with these. The extent of my knowledge is my own personal use of my family renting a beach house or condo for a week most summers. I believe vacation rentals can also be a lucrative investment.

As with any investment, you have to run the numbers and see what works. The short-term rental market is much more management-intensive as people are moving in and out every few days as opposed to every few years. Some cities and counties have ordinances restricting short-term rentals, so that needs to be taken into account. The other downside is that you must furnish these units and clean them between every new occupant. All of this comes at an expense, but often the cleaning fee can be passed along to the renter. If you hire a property management firm, the fees are higher for short-term rentals because it takes more time and energy to operate. These websites like AirBnb.com and VRBO.com typically handle security deposits, transferring funds, and a lot of the administrative things, so it can make that part easier for you.

If you are thinking about short-term rentals, you must decide if you have the time to stay on top of it or if you will hire it out. Then figure the expenses, expected vacancies, and run the numbers to see if it's worth it to you. After running these numbers, you might decide a straight lease for at least 12 months is the way to go. For me, it certainly is! I like my investment properties to be as hands-off and simple as possible. I like the cash flow with very little of my personal time involved.

But, for certain properties and certain locations, I think a short-term rental is definitely worth considering and could be the best choice. A colleague of mine has rented out condos in Athens on a short-term basis and doubled the income he would have received on a straight lease. However, this has also come at the cost of increased time and effort on his part.

LEASE/PURCHASE AND LEASE/OPTION

Lease with a purchase or lease with the option to purchase is another tactic some investors use that works well. This is also sometimes referred to as Rent-To-Own. This strategy works when they have intentions of owning properties for a short while and selling them. Some actually use it in hopes of making a little more money from the tenants, and some use it to shift more responsibility to the tenant to care for the property.

I've encountered many people who think a lease/purchase contract and a lease/option contract are the same thing. They are not. Either of these lease strategies can work well if you want to sell the property to the tenant in a year to three years, but you need to know how they work and know the difference so that you use the right one.

A lease/purchase contract is just what it sounds like. It's a lease and a purchase contract. By structuring it this way, the lease defines the monthly rent payment, term, etc. The purchase contract is a real estate contract that binds the tenant to purchasing the property for an agreed upon price by at a certain date in the future. Typically, it's one to five years out. If the buyer/tenant doesn't close, the seller can take legal action or keep earnest money. It obligates the buyer/tenant to completing the purchase, or they are in default of the contract.

A lease/option is simply a lease, and the buyer has an option contract to purchase. They typically pay an option fee. The option fee essentially buys the buyer/tenant the option or choice to purchase the property at some point in the future at a price that's agreed to when the option money is paid. The owner also cannot legally sell to anyone else even if a higher offer is made. The tenant locks up the property by purchasing the option. This option fee is kept by the seller, whether or not the buyer/tenant decides to move forward with the purchase.

Each structure could apply in different situations depending on what you are trying to accomplish. With both, I've seen structures where tenants may get credits each month that they pay on time and that goes toward the closing costs or a discount off of the final price at closing. If the buyer doesn't close, the seller/landlord keeps it all and the tenant either moves out or they both agree to extend the lease. I've not personally used this structure, but my clients have and they've shared with me that tenants have more pride of ownership in this situation, take better care of the property, and will actually repair and improve the property because in their mind it's theirs. Since they know that they will be buying it in the near future, it's already theirs in their mind.

Another thing to know is that a large portion of lease/purchase and lease/option contracts don't close. Some investors use this as a strategy. They actually hope it doesn't close, so they keep the earnest money or option money, and then repeat the process in a few years. Basically, they sell the same house over and over to different people. However, when they do close, it truly can be a win-win for both parties.

There is a reason most don't close. The tenants that enter this kind of agreement typically do so because they have aspirations of home ownership, but for some reason can't qualify for a loan. If they can qualify, then they just go get a loan and buy. I've learned that if they don't qualify due to starting a new business, being self-employed or not employed long enough, but their credit is good, the odds of closing are high. If they don't qualify for financing because of a low credit score, chances are they will never close. If they have bad credit today, it will most likely still be bad in a few years. It's bad habits that get them in the situation of bad credit, so unless they are willing to change their habits, it won't improve. And most people don't have the discipline to change habits. On some occasions, buyers with bad credit will work with a lender or advisor to improve their credit and they actually do close. Some of them just don't have the discipline to change bad habits.

Options can also work when you are purchasing property. It's not usually needed and not usually the best way to do it, but it can work in certain situations. It's just something to be familiar with and have in your tool belt should the need arise. If you are willing to gamble the option fee, you can buy yourself some time to decide whether or not you really want to move forward on a deal. If you don't move forward, you don't get your option money back in this situation.

Lease/purchase and lease/option structures are more sophisticated ways of doing real estate, so I recommend you do more study, get more education, and find a mentor if this is a structure you want to use in your business. Many people have had great success doing it.

Personally, I'm not a fan of rent-to-own agreements in most cases. I don't want to keep a tenant's option money or earnest money because they can't perform when I knew the odds of them performing were slim in the beginning. To me, it's taking advantage of them a little bit. But also, I don't typically want to lock myself into selling a house to a tenant in a few years. What if the market gets really hot, and the property goes way up in value? Then you sell yourself short.

I actually once had a client who entered into a lease/purchase agreement with a tenant/buyer. This was during the economic downturn when it was hard to sell homes. It had been on the market a few months without selling, and the owner had already moved. The interested buyer approached us about a lease/purchase, and the owner thought it would be a good idea. This particular buyer was actually self-employed and had just opened a new business. His credit score was good, but he didn't have the work history and years of income needed to get a loan at the present time. I knew the odds were good it would close in a few years. The seller wanted to sell the house, so I was not opposed to the idea. The problem was that the seller was willing to negotiate and enter into a contract for a lower-than-list price and close in three years. The real estate market at this time was on its way back up.

My advice to the seller (who I was representing) was to only agree at list price or maybe more because the market was starting to improve and it would be worth more in three years. However, he was motivated and wanted to move forward, so he reduced his price. And that's OK. It was his house and his decision to make.

This one did close at the scheduled time, and I remember thinking at that time that the tenant was getting a great deal and instant equity. The lease/purchase worked in favor of the tenant. The market had indeed risen, and had the seller been selling on the open market at that time, he would have been able to sell for more. Nevertheless, the seller was happy because he was getting rid of a house he didn't want and he had received rent payments each month for 3 years. In the end, this was a win-win because the seller had peace of mind, a payment each month to cover the mortgage, and got the sale he was looking for. The tenant ended up with a great deal on a house with equity.

OWNER FINANCING

Another sophisticated approach is owner financing. With owner financing, instead of the buyer getting a loan from the bank, the person selling the house lends the buyer the money for the purchase. The seller conveys the property to the buyer just like a regular sale, but the seller simply becomes the bank in this situation.

Owner financing will probably not be an option for you unless you own your properties free and clear and you want to sell them. I see this strategy used by investors who are ready to start cashing out on their properties.

They may decide to retire to the beach or the mountains or whatever. They are tired of managing the properties, so rather than continue to be the owner and landlord, they sell them and become the bank.

They like this strategy because they now are simply receiving payments, just like a bank, but they no longer have to worry about covering the expenses of management, making repairs, etc. If the buyer/tenant doesn't make a payment, the seller/owner can foreclose and take the house back.

Remember, selling with owner financing is kind of like a dairy selling their milk cows. You've owned the property for years, and it's continued to pump cash into your bank account. Once you start selling, over a period of time, that monthly cash flow will dry up. Sure, the bank account is bigger, but the monthly cash flow will eventually go away.

Think about a dairy that sells the cows. The bank account gets larger, but the revenue from the milk each day/week/month is gone.

In my opinion, once you get the properties paid for, just continue to let them pump money to you. If you don't want to deal with management, hire a professional firm and continue to own and rent the property. Then your heirs can also enjoy the cash flow that you've put in place for them.

Don't get me wrong. I'm not completely opposed to selling. Sometimes you need to sell so you can upgrade and continue to grow your portfolio as previously discussed. My advice is to make sure when you sell, if possible, that you replace it with a better property.

Owner financing can be right in some situations, and investors that I know who do it like it. It works well for them. They can get 8% to 12% on their money, and they are happy. It's secured by the real estate, so it's like a guaranteed return. I think the investors like it too because they no longer have to deal with repairs. If the borrower doesn't pay, they can foreclose and take the house back just like a bank can. However, by straight leasing you can obtain these returns while also retaining the asset (the house) so that it can continue paying you forever. When you do owner finance, you are divesting of the assets. Each person has to decide the right strategy. The same strategy is not right for everyone.

There are many options on what kind of leases you can use and how you can structure your leases. For most, it will be a simple straight lease, for others a lease/purchase or lease/option, and for others owner financing rather than leasing. However, you need to determine which is the right choice for you. As long as you have a good solid lease agreement with good tenants, you'll be able to survive and even thrive regardless of whether the real estate prices are going up or down, which leads us to the next chapter.

CHAPTER 16
Riding the Ups and Downs

If you owned property or had anything at all to do with the real estate market from 2007 to the present, then you know firsthand that markets change. We probably saw more change in real estate prices during that decade than any other decade in history. I know for me, personally, I'm amazed at how quickly the market fell and how quickly it recovered. That market swing bankrupted many and made multimillionaires out of others.

Let's just get it out there—markets change! And they will always change. Sometimes they go up, and sometimes they go down.

Does this mean that we should try to time the market with our real estate investments? Maybe. But, as you are learning in this book, if you buy at the right price and for the right reasons and you get the return you desire on your investment, market timing doesn't matter as much. Focus on getting your desired return on investment!

Yes, I agree, buying homes in 2011 was much better than buying homes in 2007 or 2018. It's easy to see looking backward. The problem is that when you are in the current time, you are constantly asking yourself, "Is this the top of the market?" or "Is this the bottom of the market?" What's the future market going to do? The reality is that there is no way for you to know that answer while you are in the current time.

The last market crash was a lot harder, a lot faster, and a lot longer than anyone expected. So, many waited on the bottom to buy, and they didn't buy at the bottom. Then as the market started to rise, people began to wonder, "Will it continue rising?" Of course, it did continue. And some of these people are still sitting on the sideline trying to figure out what the market is going to do. Don't be one of those! Don't get analysis paralysis! Take action! Find deals where the numbers work and that give you the rate of return you are looking for, and then make the investment!

The real estate market will fall again at some point, and it will rise again at some point. However, due to inflation, demand for housing, and rising costs of building materials, housing values should rise over a long period of years.

The takeaway: stop waiting to buy real estate. Find a deal where the numbers work and buy it. If the numbers work, you can't go wrong. Try to buy slightly below value, and buy so that you get the required return on your investment and watch it grow.

There is an adage, **"Don't wait to buy real estate. Buy real estate and wait!"** It's good advice. Over time, you'll be glad you did.

ABOUT DOWN MARKETS

So, if you make a real estate investment only to learn the next year the market has gone down and it's worth less, how will that impact you? Does that mean you lost money? No! If you sell it, you will lose money. If you keep it and continue to rent it and continue to receive income each month, you will continue making money. The value at any given moment is irrelevant unless you are trying to leverage to borrow money or you need to sell. I think too many property owners freaked out during the last downturn, sold, and lost money or just gave up to foreclosure. Those that weathered the storm by renting out their homes came out great and are reaping the benefits now.

Will rents get lower in a down economy? Perhaps. But, if they do, they shouldn't change much. And they may actually go up as the demand for rentals rises. In the last recession, as people lost their homes, they became renters, so rental rates really didn't change that much for homes in most areas because the demand was strong.

Even if rents do dip a little bit, as long as you have a buffer in your cash flow, you continue making money. It's all market-driven. **In my opinion, residential real estate will remain safe because people will always need a place to live.** They will always need a place to stay dry when it rains, warm when it's cold, and cool when it's hot. Housing will be a bigger priority to people than a new car or some new clothes or whatever else when they have limited resources.

Leasing commercial real estate can be much harder during a recession as more businesses are folding and there is less demand for the space. The same is true for vacation and short term rentals during a recession. Less demand means lower prices. If you are concerned with a market downturn, in my opinion, stick with residential homes in high demand areas!

Forget Timing

I'm always watching the market. If I think it's getting ready to cool off, I may be more cautious when I buy. I may want to hold onto some cash to be ready to buy better deals in a softer market. If I think the market is going to continue rising, I may buy more aggressively. That could be called "timing the market," but I can't predict the future nor can anyone else. We don't know for sure what the market will do. The reality is that I will buy regardless of the market being up or down, if the return on investment is good and if I have the resources to do so.

The point is, if the deal is right, there is no right or wrong timing. Buy for cash flow. Always buy for cash flow. Too many people try to buy for appreciation. Consider appreciation a bonus. If the cash flow is there, real estate is very forgiving, and even if you do make mistakes, most will work themselves out over time. Most people make mistakes when they panic. Buy for cash flow, settle in for the long term, and let the money flow in each month.

To minimize risk when markets go up and down, remember the following:

1. Always buy for cash flow. Personally, I like to buy with at least $200 to $300 per month per property. Or 20% to 30% of the rent. It's highly unlikely that rent would dip more than that, even in a bad recession. By having a buffer, your risk is mitigated. Rents should rise over time giving you even more margin in the future.

2. Don't overleverage.

3. Paying your properties off puts you in a very conservative position with very little risk of losing a property or going bankrupt. It gives peace of mind!

4. Don't freak out and sell when the value goes down if the market as a whole is going down—as long as you are cash flowing. If your individual neighborhood is going down due to high crime or something negative and you think it will continue going down, then get out and upgrade to a better property. Otherwise, continue to enjoy the cash flow.

5. When the market is down, deals can be found more easily. Don't be scared to buy. Save money and be ready for it.

6. Sell a few and pay off others or refinance when the market is up.

Just remember, look at appreciation as a bonus and know that sometimes it's a big bonus. Buy for cash flow and focus on maximizing your return on investment through rent. You maximize your return by buying at the right price, minimizing repairs, and keeping a tenant in the property at all times. If the property needs repair, you need to buy at a lower price.

When you get this part right, buying the right properties at the right prices, then leasing to the right tenants and managing them and the property properly, your portfolio will grow and you'll achieve financial freedom faster than you ever thought possible.

CHAPTER 17
Finding Freedom Faster

Your goal may or may not be to "retire," but it should be financial freedom and getting there as soon as you can. Personally, I don't think I'll ever officially retire. I can't sit still and will always want to be active in some kind of pursuit.

Once you reach that goal of financial freedom and you have more income coming in passively from your investments than you do from your job, then you are financially free. You no longer NEED that job to pay your bills. You can quit if you want to or keep it if you want to. At this point, you have options.

What are some strategies to get there faster? To get to a place where you no longer have to go to work in order to pay bills? How fast you get there all depends on your current lifestyle, your income, and what you want your lifestyle to look like in the future.

If you can figure out how to live off of half your household income now, you should be able to get to that level of passive income in less than 10 years if you can generate at least a 10% return. And you should be able to double that passive income in less than 15 years if you invest aggressively and wisely. If you can generate enough additional income, you can get there much faster, in as little as few years.

It can be difficult to live off of half your household income if you have been living off of all of it up to now. However, it can be done by lowering your expenses, reducing your standard of living, getting a second job, or a spouse getting a job if they aren't currently working. It can also be done by finding a higher paying job or starting a business.

How do you find a higher paying job? Become more valuable to the marketplace. Sharpen your skills. Earning more and starting a business is beyond the scope of this book, but sharpen your skills, learn new skills, and be entrepreneurial. And if you are in commission sales, you have no excuse! Go sell more!

In the United States, the possibilities are endless. There are tons of great resources out there on this topic of becoming more valuable to the market place and earning more money. It doesn't come easy, but opportunity is there if you are willing to put in the hard work that's necessary.

EYES ON THE REAL PRIZE

I want to issue a word of caution about your quest to gain wealth. Do not sacrifice your family in order to take this journey faster. What I mean is don't forego family vacations just so you can invest a little more each year into real estate. Don't work so much overtime that you miss your child's football game, the school play, or dance recital. Spend time with your family! They are and always will be worth more than any amount of money you can make or any piece of real estate you can buy.

I'm a very driven individual, and I set high goals and work hard to achieve them. I set high financial goals, so I can give to my family. But, I've learned they just want me to give of myself and my time, and not my money. I have to keep myself in check on this. I imagine the same is true of what your family wants and expects from you.

Don't focus so much on working and investing that you sacrifice your health. Eat right and exercise. You only have one body so treat it right.

It's what's going to give you the strength and endurance to see your financial plans through to the end.

Finally, don't neglect your spiritual and personal growth. Continue to spend time learning and growing as a person. Spend time in prayer and meditation. It's easy to get so busy that life just flies by and I think we can miss out on so much that God wants to show us and teach us.

Slow down and take longer on the journey. It's OK. You'll get there. For most of us, we want financial freedom, so we'll have more time to spend with our loved ones and doing what we want with our time. So, make sure you don't lose your loved ones, your health, or your sanity in the process of getting to freedom.

Once you start investing, it will begin to snowball. But, it would be better for you to take a few extra years to achieve financial freedom than to lose the more important things in the process. If you become financially free and you are able to do what you want when you want, but lose your family, health or spirituality in the process, have you really accomplished anything worthwhile? I think not.

KEY MARKERS ON THE FAST LANE TO FREEDOM

How soon can you reach a point that you are no longer dependent on that J.O.B.?

It depends. Decide on what kind of lifestyle you want to live, how much you want to give, and how much you'll need to pay your expenses each month. Let's examine some key points on your journey to financial freedom through real estate investing.

Passive Cash Flow

Once your passive cash flow is at least one dollar higher than your monthly expenses, you are technically financially free. However, I don't recommend you quit your job at this time. Not yet.

My recommendation is to continue working for a while to let your cash flow continue to grow so that you have excess each month. Continue doing what you have been doing. Continue to increase your income. The more you make, the more you can invest, the more you can give and help others, and the more you can contribute to society.

Debt-Free

I also recommend you be debt-free to really be free. Remember, according to Proverbs 22:7, the borrower is servant to the lender, so can you really be "free" if you are a servant to a lender? I think not.

Once you are debt-free and have passive income to cover all of your expenses, you'll have more choices on how to spend your time. You won't be tied to your work in the same way, and you'll find that you may want to take more time off and spend more time enjoying other activities.

Monthly Income

Determine what you'll need monthly in order to always be able to pay your bills, even if expenses rise. Most likely, whatever you decide to do with your time will cause your expenses to rise. If it's a hobby, there will be new expenses. If it's travel, there will be additional expenses. If you decide to start a new business, there will be expenses. If you choose to do volunteer or mission work, you'll want to be able to give to those you are helping and be able to contribute more than just your time.

Figure out the amount you'll need each month to live your lifestyle of choice after you are debt-free. Will you need $3,000 per month, $5,000, $10,000, $20,000? This number will be different for everyone. It will be different depending on where you live and your lifestyle. Obviously, the smaller the number, the faster you can reach it.

If your expenses will be $5,000 per month, and you have $5,000 in cash flow coming in from your rental property, technically, you are free. However, you are setting yourself up for failure if you don't build that number higher. I suggest at least 50% higher, and ideally, double it!

Why? It needs to be higher than your monthly expenses simply to create margin. If there's no margin, then an unexpected repair, a vacancy, or your need to purchase a new automobile will set you back. If you've come this far, you don't want to go backwards! Quitting your primary income stream too early will be a setback.

MARGIN

Why do I recommend doubling your monthly cash flow? So that you have enough margin you can cover unexpected expenses, but also so you can continue to invest! Imagine what it would look like if your expenses were $5,000 per month, but you were bringing in $10,000 per month passively. Then, you've got an extra $60K per year to invest or to give away to your favorite charity or mission project if you don't need it. But, to need it and not have it would send you back to work and slaving away again for a paycheck.

GROWTH

Why in the world would you work so hard to get yourself into a position of freedom and stop doing what you did to get there? That's just not smart. Once you begin to live off your cash flow, you still need to live off of half of what you bring in so that you can invest the other half and continue to grow your wealth. Continue the upward trajectory. I'm a big believer in giving and supporting missions and charities as well. When you have a surplus of income, you have opportunities to help others in ways that you would not otherwise have.

FREEDOM

It's nice to know that you now have the freedom of choice, and you can continue working or not. If you quit your job, that's fine. However, I recommend that you don't completely stop working. "Retirement" is an American term, and I don't really see it throughout history or in Scripture. I believe that human beings are made to be in pursuit. We are made to pursue God and other humans in relationships. We are made to be creative as God was creative when He made the world. I think when you stop being creative, working, or pursuing, then you stop feeling alive. You are no longer doing what you were made to do.

ACTIVE AND ENGAGED

Imagine what it will be like when you achieve the goal. You will have the freedom to pursue whatever your heart desires. You can work on that passion or hobby that you think about all the time. You can do mission work. You can volunteer. You can pick up a new hobby. You can travel more and basically do whatever you want. You can build a business or continue to invest in real estate. Keep your mind occupied, and don't fall into idleness.

In 2 Thessalonians 3, Paul admonishes the people to work, not be idle, and to earn their own living. If you've worked hard enough to reach financial freedom, you've earned your living. I believe you can refocus your priorities, but don't become idle. Stay active!

Pat Hiban, once a top-producing real estate agent and the author of *6 Steps to 7 Figures: A Real Estate Professional's Guide to Building Wealth and Creating Your Own Destiny*, was able to retire at age 46 to never have to work again. He invested his commission income into houses, apartments, and commercial property. However, he also has not become idle. He now spends his time doing podcasts and producing educational content and online courses for other real estate agents to help them to be better at their careers and to sell more houses. If you are a real estate agent, check out his podcast, *Real Estate Rockstars*.

Another investor I know owns several houses with lots of passive cash flow. He spends his time contracting to do work on houses for other people because he enjoys it.

Personally, I have enough passive income from my real estate investments to cover my basic living expenses. So, while I could quit working and survive, I'm still running my real estate brokerage, acquiring more properties, paying down debt, and working to complete the goal of being truly financially free: being debt-free while continuing to increase my passive income. I'm not ready to slow down yet. I think if I quit, something inside of me would die. I thrive on the pursuit of growing and being the best that I can be. I enjoy training and coaching the agents in my brokerage to be better. I also enjoy seeing our clients get sound advice and make wise real estate decisions. I want to keep using what I've been given to help others. I also still have some debt on real estate to pay off before I will consider myself completely "free." Even then, I won't stop contributing, working, helping others to grow and growing myself.

Throughout my life, I've seen individuals work hard for a company, save money, and put all of their efforts to reach the goal of "retirement." Then, they stop working and start sitting around the house. What happens next? Their health starts to decline, and they die.

When you reach the awesome position of financial freedom, don't stop and become idle. Just let it be a new chapter in your life. If you aren't working for your job because you have the income, donate your time to a non-profit or to volunteering. Go do mission work or provide aid after natural disasters. Contribute your time and efforts to improve the world.

PORTRAIT OF YOUR SNOWBALL

Once you achieve financial freedom, your strategy may change from the early years. If you continue working and living off the income from your job and allowing your cash flow to continue to stack up, then you can also easily continue to add properties as well.

Let me paint the picture for you on how fast it can grow and how fast it can snowball. If you keep your current standard of living throughout the years on your journey to freedom, your income will grow rapidly and you'll be able to drastically increase the amount of income from your investments.

For example, let's say you earn $80K per year from your job and for years you have been allocating $20K of that salary to invest in real estate. You have invested long enough that you now have $5,000 per month coming in from your investments. That's $60K per year from your investments so you have replaced what you need to live on and could stop working. However, by continuing to work, you will have a total of $80K per year you can invest. If you quit your job, you'll only be living off of $60K from the rental property and have nothing left to continue investing. And you would have no margin so it's a dangerous way to live. By continuing to work a little longer, you could keep buying properties with your cash flow and the excess from your job. You could take the $80K and buy more houses. You could even pay cash for a house every one to two years if you wanted to remain conservative.

Then your income would grow by another $12,000 or so each year, meaning that you would have an extra $92K to invest the following year. That means you could buy another house even faster.

You could even get into commercial property or multifamily homes if you so choose. However, I recommend having at least half of your assets and half of your monthly income to come from single-family homes. That's just my opinion and not everyone will agree with me. I like single-family homes best because they are desirable to most people, they rent easily, and they sell easily. In my opinion, they are one of the most stable of the real estate asset classes. For added security, keep the ones that are in the most desirable locations.

Your freedom can come really fast once you have cash flow that's equivalent to your annual salary and you continue to invest it. Then, don't stop until you have more than you need. Continue to invest and your wealth will continue to grow even though you are no longer going to your job every day.

My personal rules before quitting your primary job or retiring:

1. Be debt-free.

2. Have passive net income that's 1.5 to 2 times your living expenses.

3. Have at least half of your assets in single-family residences.

Once you are financially free, you can choose how to spend your time each day. You can do what you feel you are called to do to make a real impact in the world. You can even keep working while continuing to grow your wealth. The point—you are free! Free to choose what you want to do.

So, when you reach financial freedom, what are your plans? What will you do with your newfound time? Stop reading and just think on that for a minute . . .

The real question: do you believe that you can do it? Do you believe that you can reach financial freedom? Your belief or non-belief in yourself and your ability to make it happen will dictate whether or not it actually happens.

If you don't believe in yourself and your ability to execute the real estate investment strategies given in this book, you will never achieve financial freedom. It's all about your mindset, so you've got to get that part right! Because of its crucial importance, the closing chapter is dedicated to mindset—you getting your mindset right.

CHAPTER 18
Making It Happen: Mindset

You now have the information and a plan for financial freedom through real estate. Whether or not you reach that goal of financial freedom will come down to whether or not you have the belief in yourself that you can do it and the discipline to put forth the work and effort required to reach it. It's simple, but it's not easy. It is certainly possible, and plenty of people have proven it. Now it's time to prove it to yourself by believing you can do it!

I hope you can now see a path to how it can be done and know that it's possible for you. Ultimately, your success is up to you. No one else can do it for you. How bad do you want it? Do you want to be free in the future and are you willing to make some sacrifices and take some calculated risks now in order to make it a reality? By being diligent for a few years, it can pay off in a huge way a few more years into the future.

Now it's up to you and what you do with this information. Your mindset will be a large contributor as to whether you actually achieve your goal.

TIPS FOR HITTING GOALS

I want to close by giving you some tips on how to remain consistent and intentional about hitting your goals.

First, decide what is reasonable based on the income you are making now and how much you will have to invest once you make the necessary changes.

Next, decide how many houses you can buy with that amount of money. That will depend on the real estate market where you are buying and whether you want to pay cash or use debt and put 20% down. Remember, you'll typically need at least 20% down unless you choose the non-traditional means of purchasing.

Once you've made those determinations, it's time you map out a plan. Sit down right now, take out a sheet of paper, or open a document on your computer. Work on a budget and savings plan. Be sure to address the following:

- How much can you save each year to invest?

- How can you earn additional income to invest?

- How many houses will you buy each year?

I would encourage you to figure out a way to buy at least one house per year. If not one per year, one every other year or one as often as you can. The bottom line: set a goal and stay focused on it.

YOU, ME & MARK

I've seen people from all walks of life produce a consistent monthly income with real estate. Think about people you know. You may know some of these people as well. Don't think my investment plan is just for the super humans, mega-rich, or big time geniuses. If so, I would be disqualified. It's normal people, just like you and me, who are finding financial freedom through real estate.

Let me tell you about a client of mine, who we'll call Mark. Mark is on his way to financial freedom with real estate. He is in his thirties. He paints houses for a living and is rapidly paving his way to financial freedom. He bought his first house from us just a few years ago. We are now managing two homes for him that he bought with cash (i.e., no mortgages). We're doing the management because he wants to focus on his painting business and doesn't want to even think about his rental homes. Mark lives frugally, saves his money, and is looking forward to a brighter future for himself and his family.

I have a tremendous amount of respect for Mark. He is really living out Dave Ramsey's advice of "Live now like no one else, so you can really LIVE later like no one else." Reality is though, Mark doesn't live like a miser. He lives in a nice house and drives a nice vehicle in addition to his work van. He does work a lot but still makes time to be with his wife and children. He's built a great business that produces excess money that he can invest into real estate for passive income.

We consistently deposit almost $2,400 into Mark's bank account each month from his two investment properties. That's money he makes that he doesn't have to go to work to earn. The homes are now worth quite a bit more than what he paid for them just a few years ago. He bought these houses at a good price and made general improvements after buying them, so they rarely have repair issues to come up. This makes his monthly revenue pretty consistent. He's allowing this revenue to build, and he recently told me he's about ready to buy another property. He will soon have three homes with no mortgages that will continue to pump money out to him. He's not yet 40 years old.

Do you think Mark can stop painting for a living in the near future? Yes, he can if he so chooses. He is living out the financial freedom real estate investment plan I've explained in this book.

If Mark can do it, and if I can do it, then you can too!

What are you waiting for? Get started!

Remember, "Don't wait to buy real estate. Buy real estate and wait."

Also I already pointed out, a support team helps tremendously in getting you to financial freedom faster. If you are in the Athens, GA area, my team and I are ready to be a part of your team. You can find us on:

- www.WoodallRealtyGroup.com

- www.Facebook.com/woodallrealtygroup

If you are buying property in this area, my team and I can help you to select the right properties to reach your goals.

If you are buying elsewhere in the United States or abroad, chances are, we can connect you with an agent in that area that is knowledgeable about investment real estate. Some of these agents may have even been through our training program. For a referral, go to www.TheReal EstateWayBook.com/findagent

I've lived the stories and examples in this book. While I know a lot about real estate, I don't know it all. One of Woodall Realty Group's core values is to be growth-minded. That means we are always trying to learn new things and grow as individuals and as a company. I don't think I'll ever stop learning new things. But, just learning something new is not enough. You must take action on what you learn! Now, it's your turn. Take action and change your future with this information!

Again, my team and I are here to help, and we can be reached in the following ways:

- To learn more about investing in real estate, go to www.TheRealEstateWayBook.com

- To buy or sell in the Athens, Georgia area, go to www.Woodall RealtyGroup.com.

- For property management in the Athens, Georgia area, go to www.IronHorsePropertyManagement.com.

EPILOGUE
Beyond Retirement

The whole premise of this book has been learning what you can do today to improve your future through investing in real estate. I hope this book has helped you to develop a plan for a brighter future in your life so that you can fund your dreams and your retirement. However, one day we'll be gone, so this epilogue is about planning even further into the future… into eternity. While your wealth will be left behind, you can live forever. And, you can even have treasure forever.

Jesus said in Matthew 16:26, "For what will it profit a man if he gains the whole world and forfeits his soul?" I feel I would be remiss if I write an entire book about investing and creating a brighter future on this earth while not including my beliefs about eternal life, Heaven, and how you can have freedom forever!

In John 14:6, Jesus said "I am the way, and the truth, and the life. No one comes to the Father except through me." Scripture tells us that Jesus is the one and only Son of God.

THE BAD NEWS

Throughout history and in Scripture, both in the Old Testament and the New Testament, it's clear that all people, you and I included, have broken God's laws and sinned against him. Our ancestors did and we have too. For example, have you ever lied, stolen, used God's name in vain, committed adultery, put other things ahead of God? These are just a few of the ten commandments. If you have broken any of them (God's law), then you are a sinner (me too).

However, even though we all fail, God wants to be in fellowship with us and wants us to live! We are made in His image. He is relational just as we are relational. But because He is perfect and just, He can't fellowship with us when we have sinned against Him. And because He is a God of justice, He also can't simply forgive us and overlook our sin and still remain just. To be just, He must punish us for our sin, in a similar way that our society punishes lawbreakers. (You do want someone who burglarizes your house or murders someone to be punished, right? To receive justice for their crimes?) For a judge to simply overlook someone's crime would be unjust. God is not unjust, because He is perfect. So, He must punish our disobedience to him (breaking his laws), even the ones that we consider small or insignificant. They are not insignificant to God. As it has been from the beginning of time, the punishment for sin is death forever separated from God. (Romans 6:23)

THE GOOD NEWS

That's where Jesus, God's son, comes in. He came to this earth as God in a human body. He's the part of God's plan that reconciles us as humans back to God. Jesus lived on this earth as a human, just like you and me. However, He never sinned and never broke any of God's commands. Hebrews 4:15 tells us that Jesus was tempted just as we are, yet He was without sin. Jesus didn't deserve to die! He was without sin! Yet, He allowed himself to be killed and He died as our substitute. He paid the price of death for us. When He was crucified, He exclaimed "My God, my God, why have you forsaken me?" (Matthew 27:46). God the Father turned His back on His own son, accepting His death on the cross as payment for the sins that you and I have committed. Jesus was then raised back to life after three days.

The Bible says that if we repent and put our faith in Christ, we will be saved. Romans chapter four explains that when we believe in Jesus, our faith is counted as righteousness and our sins forgiven. Once we do that, we will have eternal life. We will have new desires as we seek to follow Him and serve Him. And not only will He give us eternal life with Him in Heaven, but He will give us strength to live this life on earth with a peace that is beyond understanding. To know that your sins are forgiven, that God loves you enough to die for you, and that although your body will die, you will live forever in Heaven with Him gives unbelievable peace and joy. To know that to die without Christ and without forgiveness should make anyone fearful.

I encourage you to seek God out if you haven't already and seek for the truth and life that is found through Jesus Christ. The book of John and Romans in the New Testament are good places to start.

After finding peace with God, I encourage you to use your resources and your wealth to bless others. Bring glory to God on this earth and lay up your treasure in Heaven. I hope to see you there one day!

REFERENCES
Book Endnotes

1. J. D. Roth, "How Much Does the Stock Market Return?" Get Rich Slowly, November 21, 2018, https://www.getrichslowly.org/stock-market-returns/.

2. Caroline O'Hara, "How Much Money Do I Need to Retire?" AARP, accessed December 5, 2018, https://www.aarp.org/work/retirement-planning/info-2015/nest-egg-retirement-amount.html.

3. Todd Campbell, "Are Your Retirement Savings Keeping Pace with the Average American's?" The Motley Fool, March 16, 2018, accessed December 5, 2018, https://money.cnn.com/2018/03/16/retirement/average-retirement-savings/index.html.

4. "How to Plan for Rising Health Care Costs," Fidelity, April 18, 2018, accessed December 5, 2018, https://www.fidelity.com/viewpoints/personal-finance/plan-for-rising-health-care-costs.

5. Catherine Schnaubelt, "Planning for the High Cost of Healthcare in Retirement," Forbes, June 6, 2018, https://www.forbes.com/sites/catherineschnaubelt/2018/06/06/planning-for-the-high-cost-of-healthcare-in-retirement/#24327445513d.

6. Neel Burton, "Our Hierarchy of Needs," Psychology Today, May 23, 20012, https://www.psychologytoday.com/us/blog/hide-and-seek/201205/our-hierarchy-needs.

7. Abigail Summerville, "There Are More Renters Than Any Time Since 1965," July 20, 2017, https://www.cnbc.com/2017/07/20/there-are-more-renters-than-any-time-since-1965.html.

8. Kirsten Weir, "Delaying Gratification," in "What You Need to Know about Willpower: The Psychological Science of Self-Control,"

American Psychological Association, 2012, 3–4, https://www.apa.org/helpcenter/willpower.pdf.

9. Engelo Rumora, "How to Evaluate A-Class, B-Class, and C-Class Properties," Biggerpockets.com, accessed December 16, 2018, https://www.biggerpockets.com/renewsblog/evaluate-asset-classes/.

10. U.S. Bureau of the Census and U.S. Department of Housing and Urban Development, Median Sales Price of Houses Sold for the United States (MSPUS), retrieved from FRED, Federal Reserve Bank of St. Louis, accessed December 16, 2018, https://fred.stlouisfed.org/series/MSPUS.

11. "Median and Averages Sales Prices of New Homes Sold in the United States," United States Census Bureau, accessed December 16, 2018, https://www.census.gov/construction/nrs/pdf/uspriceann.pdf.

Acknowledgments

I would like to thank my wife, Katie, who always challenges me and makes me better. I would not have been able to have the success I've had or to write this book without her support throughout my career.

Thanks to my parents for raising me to work and teaching me to plan for my future from an early age.

Thanks to George and John for helping me to get my start in real estate.

Thanks to my staff members, Michael and Caroline, and to Tim for reading the first draft of this book and giving me feedback.

Thanks to Nancy and to my mother for doing such a great job editing and helping me get to the finish line.

Thanks to all of our past and future real estate clients, I wouldn't have the knowledge and expertise I have without you.

Thanks to my entire team of staff and agents for supporting me and our clients well.

To my Lord and Savior, Jesus Christ, for saving me so that I can truly live.

About the Author

Justin Woodall is a licensed real estate broker in Georgia. He owns and operates Woodall Realty Group and Iron Horse Property Management, both serving the greater Athens, Georgia area. He is happily married with three children. When he's not working, he enjoys spending time with his wife and children. He also enjoys exercising, hunting, fishing, and just about anything outdoors.

If you'd like to discuss real estate investing with Justin, he'd be happy to speak to you, whether you are located in the Georgia area or another part of the US. To reach him please use the Woodall Realty Group contact information that's given below.

About Woodall Realty Group

Woodall Realty Group serves home buyers and home sellers in the Athens and north Georgia region. While they do work with investors, they primarily help the traditional buyer or seller to buy or sell their principal residences.

The company was formed by Justin Woodall who started his real estate career in 2004. After spending time at two national brokerage companies in Athens, Justin and his team of agents left to open Woodall Realty Group.

With only a few highly productive agents, Woodall Realty Group's production ranks in the top 5% of companies in the Athens area. Justin attributes these results to the quality of agents they hire, the training they provide, the unique structure of their team, and the systems they implement to give the best service possible. The team consistently outperforms the market averages.

No matter where you are located in the US, Woodall Realty Group is ready to help you invest in real estate. They are connected to professional real estate agents and investors across the US, so in addition to supplying you with advice, they can refer you to experienced experts in your area.

Woodall Realty Group's contact information:
www.WoodallRealtyGroup.com
706-621-6085
www.Facebook.com/woodallrealtygroup

If you are outside the Athens, Georgia area and are looking for a qualified real estate agent in your area, you can go to www.TheRealEstateWayBook.com/findagent.

About Iron Horse Property Management

Iron Horse Property Management is a company that was formed more recently after Justin saw the need for quality property management in the Athens area. Because Justin is passionate about income-producing real estate, primarily residential real estate, he wanted a way to serve his past clients and the Athens area with reliable management services.

If you are in the Athens area and interested in quality property management, please contact Iron Horse Property Management:

www.IronHorsePropertyManagement.com
706-395-5053
www.Facebook.com/ironhorseproperty

* * *

If this book has been meaningful and helpful to you, please take a moment to **leave a review on Amazon** so that others can benefit as well. I would greatly appreciate it!

To learn more about investing and for more tools and resources including a FREE Investment Property ROI Analyzer or to find real estate agents to help you in your area, visit:

www.TheRealEstateWay.com

Made in the
USA
Columbia, SC